Agile Project Management with GreenHopper 6 Blueprints

An intuitive guide to efficiently track and manage projects in an agile way using GreenHopper for JIRA

Jaibeer Malik

PUBLISHING

BIRMINGHAM - MUMBAI

Agile Project Management with GreenHopper 6 Blueprints

First published: August 2013

Production Reference: 2210813

Published by Packt Publishing Ltd.
Livery Place
35 Livery Street
Birmingham B3 2PB, UK.

ISBN 978-1-84969-973-0

www.packtpub.com

Cover Image by Abhishek Pandey (abhishek.pandey1210@gmail.com)

Credits

Author
Jaibeer Malik

Reviewer
David Jellison

Acquisition Editor
Vinay Argekar

Commissioning Editor
Shaon Basu

Technical Editor
Shali Sasidharan

Project Coordinator
Suraj Bist

Proofreader
Lucy Rowland

Indexer
Hemangini Bari

Graphics
Ronak Dhruv

Production Coordinator
Zahid Shaikh

Cover Work
Zahid Shaikh

About the Author

Jaibeer Malik is an experienced programmer and Agile enthusiast with a passion for new technologies, clean code, and Agile development.

He has been working in the IT industry for nearly 10 years now with extensive experience in software designing, architecture, and development in domains varying from internet to telecom, to finance, oil, gas, and transport. He is involved in the development of both small and big enterprise applications that make a difference in the real world. He has good experience in technologies such as Java, J2EE, Hibernate, Spring, Wicket, Flex, Scala, ElasticSearch, and many other open source technologies.

He is a Certified Scrum Product Owner (CSPO), Certified Scrum Master (CSM), and experienced in distributed Agile development. He regularly writes his thoughts in the form of blog posts on his personal website and on other technical forums.

He is currently located in Amsterdam, working as a Java Software Architect for one of the top e-commerce platforms in Netherlands.

To know more about the author visit the following links:

Blog: http://jaibeermalik.wordpress.com

Twitter: http://twitter.com/jaibeermalik

LinkedIn: http://www.linkedin.com/in/jaibeermalik

I would like to express my sincere thanks and gratitude to all those who provided support, encouragement, and those who pushed me a little further.

About the Reviewer

David Jellison, Director of Quality Engineering at Constant Contact (Twitter: @ConstantContact), has 20 years of experience in quality and development management and test automation development. He is a Certified Scrum Master (CSM) and is currently leading Kanban initiatives in quality engineering, project management, and continuous delivery at Constant Contact. He has driven culture change and continuous improvement in Agile practices in three different SaaS organizations. Being passionate about efficiency in product delivery, he drives continuous improvements in test automation infrastructure, test design patterns, and Agile continuous integration practices. He administrates and designs workflows, and develops add-on plugins for Jira/Greenhopper. He spoke at the Atlassian Summit 2012 and StarWest 2012, and is a co-organizer of the Greater Boston Selenium Users Group. Follow Dave's blog at davidjellison.wordpress.com and his Twitter handle is @davidjellison.

www.PacktPub.com

Support files, eBooks, discount offers and more

You might want to visit www.PacktPub.com for support files and downloads related to your book.

Did you know that Packt offers eBook versions of every book published, with PDF and ePub files available? You can upgrade to the eBook version at www.PacktPub.com and as a print book customer, you are entitled to a discount on the eBook copy. Get in touch with us at service@packtpub.com for more details.

At www.PacktPub.com, you can also read a collection of free technical articles, sign up for a range of free newsletters and receive exclusive discounts and offers on Packt books and eBooks.

http://PacktLib.PacktPub.com

Do you need instant solutions to your IT questions? PacktLib is Packt's online digital book library. Here, you can access, read and search across Packt's entire library of books.

Why Subscribe?

- Fully searchable across every book published by Packt
- Copy and paste, print and bookmark content
- On demand and accessible via web browser

Free Access for Packt account holders

If you have an account with Packt at www.PacktPub.com, you can use this to access PacktLib today and view nine entirely free books. Simply use your login credentials for immediate access.

Table of Contents

Preface

GreenHopper is an Agile Project Management tool built as add-on to Atlassian issue tracking system Jira. The rich interface of the tool allows you to focus on the work in hand and aims to achieve productivity.

It provides inbuilt support for Agile methodologies such as Scrum and Kanban. The inbuilt support for these processes makes the process adoption much easier. The flexible and customizable nature of Jira allows you to configure the tool to map to the hybrid Agile nature of the process, suiting your team requirements best.

It allows you to quickly and directly start with the backlog creation for your project. Suiting best to Scrum you can create Epic/Story/Technical task issues in a smooth and quicker way. You can prioritize your backlog items based on different business requirements. Managing prioritized backlog items and filtering capability allows you to work with both small and large backlogs.

It allows teams to estimate the backlog in an efficient and quick way. Teams can choose the estimate measurement criteria from various options. It allows planning the sprint and managing the sprint backlog efficiently. Daily sprint or Agile team tracking, transparency, and visibility have never been so easy as it is with the GreenHopper task boards. The rich interface of the task board makes it easy for team members to work on day-to-day technical tasks, prioritize items on task board well, update the task status, and so on.

The reporting functionality of GreenHopper gives enough information for any Agile project. The sprint Burndown charts, Epic reporting, and velocity charts allow you to track teams and backlogs over sprints. The control chart allows you to focus on improvements for your process. The cumulative flow diagram gives information related to how the whole backlog is moving ahead. The additional Jira reporting feature allows you to generate relevant reporting capability to your project.

What this book covers

Chapter 1, Getting Started with GreenHopper, introduces the basic Agile concepts, Scrum terminology, prerequisites, installing GreenHopper, common glossary, and rich interface features.

Chapter 2, Planning Your Sprints with GreenHopper, allows creating a Jira project, Agile board, backlog items such as Epic, Story, and technical tasks, ranking the backlog items, and creating a sprint.

Chapter 3, Estimating and Time Tracking, helps to understand estimating and time tracking, estimating using Story points, business value, ideal hours, and Tempo plugin for time tracking.

Chapter 4, Using the Work Board to Update Issues, covers working with task board, adding columns, viewing issue details, updating issue status, ranking on task board, and using keyboard shortcuts.

Chapter 5, Using Quick Filters and Highlighting Issues, explains Jira filters for board, Quick Filters, Swimlanes, and using card colors for highlighting issues.

Chapter 6, Understanding the Burndown Chart, helps you to understand Burndown chart basics, typical Burndown charts, measurements units, and scope management.

Chapter 7, Ending a Sprint, covers completing a sprint, handling unfinished sprint backlog, sprint reporting, and completing an Epic.

Chapter 8, Project Reporting Using Charts, covers Agile project reporting, velocity charts, Epic reports, control charts, and cumulative flow diagrams.

Chapter 9, Managing Kanban Team with GreenHopper, covers the Kanban system, creating a Kanban board, configuring task board columns, limiting work in progress using column constraints, creating swimlanes, ranking issues, and reporting for the Kanban team.

Appendix, Continuous Improvement, helps with the process improvements and GreenHopper tool integration points to achieve the same.

Who this book is for

The book is about managing Agile projects using the tooling system GreenHopper. It gives the brief overview of Agile process specifically Scrum and will explain step-by-step how different roles in an Agile tool can use the book in an Agile project. Any team member, project manager, product owner, Scrum master, Scrum team member (developer, designer, tester, and so on), or even the administrator can start using the tools for the project.

As a product owner or manager you will be able to plan the project. You will be able to create your project backlog, groom it over a period of time, and plan sprints tracking your milestones in the project. Using the tooling, you will be able to coordinate different team backlogs and different projects in a much smoother way.

As a Scrum master, you will be able to track and monitor the team using the tool. You will be able to work with product owners to manage and groom the backlog better and at the same time track how the team is doing using task board. Based on your situation and the dynamics of the team, you should be able to visualize the impediments better and respond to them faster.

As a team member, you will be able to track your day-to-day tasks, clarifications, impediments, dependencies, and use your work hours in a much better way. The rightly configured and adopted tooling system will minimize the effort and overheads of using it.

Using the book, readers will be able to kick start with GreenHopper in a quicker way and will be able to utilize the system fast. Within a few steps, you will be able to get started with an Agile project.

Conventions

In this book, you will find a number of styles of text that distinguish between different kinds of information. Here are some examples of these styles, and an explanation of their meaning.

New terms and **important words** are shown in bold.

Words that you see on the screen, in menus or dialog boxes for example, appear in the text like this: "Click on the **Free Trial** button to install the plugin".

 Warnings or important notes appear in a box like this.

Reader feedback

Feedback from our readers is always welcome. Let us know what you think about this book—what you liked or may have disliked. Reader feedback is important for us to develop titles that you really get the most out of.

To send us general feedback, simply send an e-mail to feedback@packtpub.com, and mention the book title through the subject of your message.

If there is a topic that you have expertise in and you are interested in either writing or contributing to a book, see our author guide on www.packtpub.com/authors.

Customer support

Now that you are the proud owner of a Packt book, we have a number of things to help you to get the most from your purchase.

Errata

Although we have taken every care to ensure the accuracy of our content, mistakes do happen. If you find a mistake in one of our books—maybe a mistake in the text or the code—we would be grateful if you would report this to us. By doing so, you can save other readers from frustration and help us improve subsequent versions of this book. If you find any errata, please report them by visiting http://www.packtpub.com/support, selecting your book, clicking on the **errata submission form** link, and entering the details of your errata. Once your errata are verified, your submission will be accepted and the errata will be uploaded to our website, or added to any list of existing errata, under the Errata section of that title.

Piracy

Piracy of copyright material on the Internet is an ongoing problem across all media. At Packt, we take the protection of our copyright and licenses very seriously. If you come across any illegal copies of our works, in any form, on the Internet, please provide us with the location address or website name immediately so that we can pursue a remedy.

Please contact us at copyright@packtpub.com with a link to the suspected pirated material.

We appreciate your help in protecting our authors, and our ability to bring you valuable content.

Questions

You can contact us at questions@packtpub.com if you are having a problem with any aspect of the book, and we will do our best to address it.

1
Getting Started with GreenHopper

Software development is fundamentally different from other similar engineering areas. The Information Technology industry has come a long way in understanding this by learning, adopting, and improving different development methodologies.

This chapter will include the following:

- Why be Agile
- The common Agile flavors
- How Scrum works
- Which tooling system to use
- Prerequisites for GreenHopper
- Installing GreenHopper
- Accessing GreenHopper
- Common uses and examples of GreenHopper
- GreenHopper glossary
- GreenHopper interface features
- An Agile project example

Being Agile

Engineering methodologies are plan-based and very much predictive in nature. The disciplined and procedural nature of engineering methodologies makes the whole software development process a bit slow and inefficient. The outcome of this has been the development of Agile methodologies. The benefit of Agile methodologies is that they are more predictive in nature, more people-oriented, and they focus on the end outcome, rather than being bureaucratic in nature.

Based on Agile survey for last few years, completed across different companies throughout the world, software development is shifting towards more successful project delivery using Agile methodologies. The wide spread adoption of Agile is a clear example of that. The percentage of successful projects using Agile processes is far greater.

Agile flavors

The word Agile usually refers to the philosophy behind software development. There are multiple flavors of Agile. Agile values and principles are put together to form the Agile Software Development Manifesto and the different Agile principles.

Agile development is an umbrella term describing several Agile methodologies. Some of the well-known methodologies are **Scrum**, **XP (Extreme Programming)**, **Crystal**, **FDD (Feature Driven Development)**, **DSDM (Dynamic Systems Development Method)**, and **Kanban**.

Each of these methodologies has a slightly different approach to implementing the core values and principles behind Agile Manifesto and principles. They all fundamentally incorporate communication, collaboration, continuous feedback, continuous testing, continuous interaction, continuous prioritization, and planning with continuous improvements to deliver solutions for a customer with changing requirements and businesses.

Scrum

Based on industry survey, the majority of Agile practitioners practice either Scrum, a combination of Scrum and XP, or a hybrid nature of Scrum to match team requirements. Scrum is a time-boxed iterative and incremental framework for Agile development process. It consists of teams, roles, events, artifacts, and rules. Let us understand each role and common artifacts in brief first.

Scrum team

The typical roles in a Scrum team are:

- **Product owner**: A product owner manages the product backlog in a prioritized form to deliver the best business value, thus grooming backlog items and helping teams with requirements and clarifications.

- **Development team**: A development team consists of self-organizing cross functional individuals (developers) working as team, who do the work in increments to deliver potentially shippable products.

- **Scrum master**: A Scrum master runs the Scrum team to make sure that Scrum theory, practices, and rules are implemented, and it works closely with the product owner, the development team, and the organization too.

Based on hybrid Scrum process, different teams also have dedicated roles for Architect and Project Manager in the team to meet specific team requirements.

Scrum events

The main Scrum events are:

- **Sprint**: A time-boxed period of nearly one month or less to deliver potentially shippable product increment based on prioritized backlog items committed by the team.

- **Sprint planning meeting**: In this, the team commits on what can be delivered from prioritized backlog items and how it will be achieved.

- **Daily Scrum**: A time-boxed daily stand-up meeting in which each team member explains what has been achieved since last meeting, what will be done before next meeting, and impediments, if any.

- **Sprint review**: In this, the team demonstrates the Sprint work and gathers feedback. It is a bi directional communication platform for the team and stakeholders on functionality delivered in a Sprint.

- **Sprint retrospective**: An opportunity for the team to introspect what went well, what needs improvement, and action items for the selected improvements.

Depending on the nature of hybrid Scrum process and team dynamics, the variations of the Scrum events, like local daily Scrum and distributed daily Scrum, are also used by various teams. Similarly, the planning and estimations process events are executed that matches best to the Scrum team requirements.

Scrum artifacts

The common Scrum artifacts are:

- **Product backlog**: An ordered list of requirements that is required in the product. It can be anything like requirements, features, enhancements, bugs, and so on.

- **Sprint backlog**: This consists of selected and ranked product backlog items planned to be delivered in a Sprint.

- **Increment**: Consists of delivered product backlog items in all earlier Sprints/Releases, and are very much usable as part of existing potentially shippable product.

Agile project management

Project management is about planning, reporting, scope, cost, risk, organizing, motivating, and managing people and resources to achieve specific goals. With Agile, the basic concept is self-organizing the team with different roles. On a Scrum project, we have roles like product owner, Scrum master, and team.

Product owner takes responsibility from the business side of the product and has the authority to make business decisions. The Scrum master acts as the team coach to remove impediments, facilitate meetings, monitor day-to-day tasks, and track project progress by performing typical project management duties. A self-organizing team is capable of working as a team to find continuous improvements.

Some of the typical tasks and requirements from an Agile project management perspective are:

- Planning and prioritizing deliveries across single or multiple teams
- Making sure backlog items are visible to everyone
- Making sure clarifications or impediments are cleared up soon
- Grooming backlog items over time
- Communicating vision and goals around team
- Planning Sprint effectively
- Tracking Sprint progress
- Long-term planning for products

- Making development process facilitation and improvements
- Working towards developing team productivity improvements
- Reporting on iteration and functionality level for better planning
- Planning roadmaps based on the work done, and the work left to do
- Increasing collaboration between team members and multiple teams

Tooling system

Agile recommends interactions over any process or tooling. Indeed, no team needs any tooling system, but using a tooling can help teams tremendously. Any tooling system we opt for should help the team to adapt to the Agile process and help in team collaboration and continuous improvement to increase productivity.

There are plenty of tools available in the market to start with Agile. On a first look at the Agile team requirements, some of the quick features you would like from a tooling system to help you are:

- Easy setting up of the Agile project
- Quick backlog creation
- Intelligent and easy backlog grooming and ranking
- Team collaboration between single and multiple teams
- Intuitive task creation and status updates
- Clear top-priority task visualization and impediment flagging
- Clear and deep reports or charting for data
- Each team member's day-to-day individual task tracking
- Easy customization and flexibility for hybrid Agile process teams
- Easy integration with business and testing teams
- Easy integration with different development and testing tools
- Easy and smooth fit for the distributed teams
- Ability to enable team to continuously improve in process and new technology integration

We will further cover how such an Agile tool like GreenHopper best fits here, mapping to all your Agile team requirements.

GreenHopper

GreenHopper is an Agile project management tool as an add-on for the well-known ticketing system **Jira** from **Atlassian**. The power of Jira allows you to customize and adapt to any hybrid Agile process matching your team requirements best. Here is the list of some of the top features of the tool which we will be covering in detail in the later chapters:

- **Agile process support** provides inbuilt support of well-known Agile methodologies like Scrum and Kanban, and is very well-equipped to support hybrid Agile process followed by your team.

- **Backlog management** supports easy, intuitive, quick creation and ranking of backlog items for your team.

- **Capacity management** supports easy and flexible estimation and time tracking process for an iteration using standard and custom field values.

- **Iteration tracking** supports easy updating of regular task status and visualizes the daily status tracking and progress of team and work.

- **Reporting and charting** allows quick and detailed reporting on iteration, functionality, and backlog items for short-term and long-term planning.

- **Continuous improvement** has an inbuilt support for team collaboration and integration with lots of development and testing tools.

- **Customization and flexibility** is the power of Jira that provides high ustomization and flexibility to your team to add support for integration of different teams and workflows, criteria, and validation of work within your organization.

Prerequisites for GreenHopper

GreenHopper is an add-on built to work with Atlassian ticketing system, Jira (http://www.atlassian.com/software/jira/overview). It is installed as a plugin on the Jira tool.

There are multiple options for you to get started with GreenHopper. For this, you can refer to http://www.atlassian.com/software/greenhopper/overview.

Atlassian offers the hosted environment for you to start using the tool. If you are already using the hosted environment for Jira, **onDemand** (http://www.atlassian. com/software/greenhopper/try/), it is easy to get started with GreenHopper also. Just "add a new product" from My Atlassian list at https://my.atlassian.com.

If you have your own maintained and installed stand-alone Jira instance, you can use Jira **Universal Plugin Manager** (**UPM**) to install the GreenHopper plugin.

Installing GreenHopper

Use the following steps to install the GreenHopper plugin in Jira using Universal Plugin Manager:

1. You need to have Jira administrator permissions to install a new plugin. Browse to **Administration** in your Jira. As shown in following screenshot, check to see the **Administration** link and click on it:

2. Select **Find New Add-ons** under the **Plugins** section on the Administration page, as shown in the following screenshot:

3. Type GreenHopper in the search box under **Atlassian Marketplace for JIRA** and press *Enter*. The plugin details will be displayed as shown in the following screenshot:

4. Click on the **Free Trial** button to install the plugin. In this book, we will be covering GreenHopper Version 6.1.x. If you are using earlier versions of GreenHopper, please upgrade to the latest version using plugin manager.

 Please note that the functionality and examples in this book are for GreenHopper Version 6.1.x.

Login to your My Atlassian account to get an evaluation license, or to buy a license and update the license information for the installed plugin.

Accessing GreenHopper

Once GreenHopper plugin has been installed successfully and the license has been updated correctly, you will see the **Agile** tab in the top navigation of your Jira system, as shown in the following screenshot:

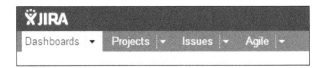

You need to exit the Administration session to see the normal logged in user view. Open the **Agile** tab to see the list of available operations to start with.

The list of boards will vary as per your board's data, as shown in the preceding screenshot. They can include:

- **Recent Boards** displays the list of recent boards you have created and you have been working with.
- **Manage Boards** allows you to configure, copy, and delete the existing boards.
- **Getting Started** allows you to get started with creating projects, boards, and with GreenHopper itself if you are starting a fresh.
- **Classic** allows you to work with earlier GreenHopper format planning and task boards. It is recommended that you use the new board style (please check Atlassian support for updates).

Common uses and examples

Jira, as a product and tooling system, has come a long way from a regular ticketing system to a powerful tool, able to manage a variety of teams and their requirements within an organization. Each organization has different departments, businesses, domains, and teams working together to achieve goals. The variation in the way of working and their requirements for each team differs. Some of the common teams working together are:

- **Development team** works with Scrum, planning backlog, updating and reporting status, and also integrates development tools. GreenHopper provides best suited toolset for your Agile development team.

- **Testing (QA) team** reports and analyzes different features, like regression and production bugs in the application, and integrates testing tools. The combination of custom workflow in Jira for your testing team, the use of the **Bonfire** testing plugin, and integration with your development team using GreenHopper works perfectly for your testing team.

- **Design team** designs the product, gets feedback from people, and forwards it to the development team to implement. The design team caters to the requirements of multiple business and development teams. Use the Kanban system for regular flow of work based on prioritization.

- **Project management team** tracks status and plans for the long run based on reporting and charting data. The mix of Jira reporting capabilities and GreenHopper charting for your teams enable project managers to track and plan the product roadmap in a much easier and better way.

- **Site operations team** works in a way similar to Kanban, to deliver maximum value and prioritize work better with high priority production issues first and future proof projects.

- **IT infrastructure team** handles team infrastructure requirements and works with the entire organization for infrastructure stability perspective. The inbuilt support of Kanban in GreenHopper helps many IT teams to work effectively.

- **Marketing and sales team** prioritizes projects, develops marketing strategy with development, design, operations team, and so on. A single platform to interact and prioritize with multiple teams enables you to plan and implement your business strategy much better.

- **Customer support team** takes end user feedback and works with development and product team, and prioritize it better. Kanban system suits the services team best, and customer support teams use GreenHopper Kanban system for the same.

One of the major requirements from any tooling system is how easily it allows coordination between all the above teams.

Jira, with all its power of customization and flexibility, allows you to make it work for varied teams. Each team can have its own customized work flow and status change condition for their day-to-day tasks and operations.

We will cover in later sections and chapters how GreenHopper can help you with the backlog management from team collaboration perspective for all the above varied teams to deliver the real business value.

For development teams, Atlassian tools suite can easily be integrated with the Jira system. Think of continuous integration build tools (**Bamboo**), online wiki for documentation (**Confluence**), source code repository integration (**Fisheye**), code review (**Crucible**) tools, and so on. All can be integrated with your backlog management tool for better tracking, visibility, and productivity.

For the testing team, to work closely with the development team to be able to verify and validate each Story and create feature bugs or regression bugs along with the Sprint itself, Jira provides testing plugin (**Bonfire**) to record testing sessions and to work closely with the development team.

In combination with Scrum, Kanban, and other hybrid Agile methodologies, GreenHopper allows you to manage teams in a much better and easier way.

GreenHopper glossary

To get started with GreenHopper, let us first get familiar with common GreenHopper terminology, which we will also be using further in this book:

- **Backlog** consists of a list of items for a product like feature, enhancements, bugs, support tickets, and so on. It can be product backlog or Sprint backlog.
- **Scrum** is an Agile development methodology to deliver in an iterative way in fixed amount of time.

- **Sprint** is an iteration in Scrum to deliver a product functionality in a time box of nearly a month or less.

- **Product backlog** is a list of requirement items for a product such as features, bugs, and so on.

- **Sprint backlog** is a list of items from product backlog picked up to deliver in a Sprint.

- **Epic** is a large functionality for the product which can further be divided into user stories to be picked up in several Sprints.

- **Story** is a conversation requirement for a part of the functionality which can be independently delivered and tested in a Sprint.

- **Task** is a technical task or subtask for a Story to be done or performed by the team members and developers to deliver a user Story.

- **Story point** is a number given to a Story to decide its relative complexity.

- **Burndown chart** is a chart to display actual and estimated amount of work, in Story points, hours or business value points over time in a particular Sprint.

- **Velocity** is the measurement of work either in Story points, custom business value, or hours that can be delivered by a team in a Sprint.

- **Kanban** is a system to reduce waste to deliver business value by controlling and limiting the work in progress.

- **Cycle time** is the time taken by an issue to change status in a flow, the time taken from work started until work finished on an issue.

- **Filter** is a query with conditions to restrict the number of issues displayed on the screen.

- **Quick filters** are configurable filters which can be stored and displayed on board to quickly filter the displayed results.

- **Swimlane** is a way of grouping and categorizing lists of issues to be displayed on the task board in horizontal bands.

GreenHopper interface features

GreenHopper provides rich interface to end users to quickly work on the backlog items and other day-to-day tasks, and other planning and reporting jobs. Some of the main interface features which make your job very easy are described in the following headings.

Single view

GreenHopper provides single board view for a team where different team activities can be achieved easily without jumping between complex navigational and browsing views, as shown in the following screenshot:

Working on the planning items view allows you to do all operations related to your backlog item like creating an item, editing an item, updating information, and attaching resources to items.

Quickly shifting between **Plan**, **Work**, and **Report** modes allows you to very easily switch to different operations.

Inline editing

GreenHopper allows inline editing of different field values.

As shown in the preceding editing screenshot, using inline editing, you would be able to edit the Story or task details on the same details screen.

Drag-and-drop

GreenHopper provides you with drag-and-drop functionality to move the items around in different panels and states.

If you are on a planning board, you can move stories around and assign it to a particular Epic. Use drag-and-drop functionality to move a Story to a particular Sprint.

If you are on a work board, you can use the drag-and-drop functionality to update the issue state.

As shown in preceding drag-and-drop screenshot, while moving tasks around, the additional feature of highlighting of states and color combination is also quite intuitive.

Quick filtering

Quick filtering and search allows users to quickly filter the all backlog items to display the desired search results.

As shown in preceding search screenshot, you can search all the backlog items to focus on your desired results.

Responsiveness

With additional improvements in the latest releases of GreenHopper related to ranking and filtering of issues, end users have the additional benefits of performance for the interface.

Using Jira filters efficiently, quick filters sensibly, and on top of that, the search functionality allows your backlog grooming very easily.

Highlighting

GreenHopper provides additional color combinations to represent different parts and functionality in a better way, that is, visually.

As shown in the preceding screenshot, you can represent different issue types with different card colors for visual representation. You can select different queries or priority-based colors for your issues.

Flexible elements

GreenHopper offers flexible panels on the view. You can show and hide different panels on the screen which you currently want to work upon, and very quickly switch between different panels.

As shown in the preceding screenshot, you can hide a panel if you are not working on it.

As shown in the preceding screenshot, you can easily close the **Details** panel on the screen if you are done updating the details for an issue.

Understandable

GreenHopper has inbuilt support for Scrum process. The terminology used within the Scrum board is inclined with the process itself. For Agile practitioners or teams starting a fresh with Agile, it is very helpful to learn the process while using the tool itself.

As shown in the preceding screenshot, different Scrum terminologies, Epics, Story, technical task, Sprint, velocity, and so on, are used to make it more understandable for your Agile team.

Intuitive

The whole interface is very intuitive for the users. The use of icons, colors, and operations are very user friendly.

As shown in the preceding screenshot, click on plus icon (**+**) to add an Epic in the backlog items. Use of relevant icons and corresponding operations make it easy for users to use the tool.

As shown in the preceding screenshot, using the right colors is intuitive enough for users. For a Sprint, estimates are displayed using three colors (red, yellow, and green). Red signifies that the work still needs to start, yellow signifies work is in progress, and green signifies that the work has already been completed.

Target audiences

Different panels and views have been implemented, keeping target audiences in focus.

Planning boards have been configured for backlog creation and grooming very quickly. All drag-and-drop functionality and estimations of Story allows product owners and Scrum masters to quickly get used to it.

Work board allows developers to update day-to-day task status and update tasks or Story relevant information on the work board itself. Additional feature of highlighting, grouping, and filtering allows you to focus on the desired results.

The reporting tab allows you to take a quick look at high-level tracking of whole Sprint and whole backlog too. Deep analysis of chart's details allows you to look at detailed information for the backlog.

The interface meets the requirements for the specific target audiences for each feature and functionality that is in place very well.

Agile project example

In this book, we will be following an example of a small business requirement which needs to be achieved through an Agile team. We will be using different screenshot examples further in this book through an example project, and will explain GreenHopper functionality along with different Agile aspects.

Project scenario

Let's say we need to develop an online photo album. We want to deliver a web version of the photo album and also a mobile version of the application, and have a site operations team to operate on that.

GreenHopper projects

Let's say we have three different teams working:

- **An Agile team for website** delivers a web version of the photo album which has its own backlog and exposing API to be used by the mobile team.

- **An Agile team for mobile** delivers a mobile version of the photo album with limited functionality and has its own backlog items.

- **A site operations team** supports online application and maintains regular infrastructure tickets in Kanban way.

Summary

In this chapter, we have become familiar with the basic idea behind Agile. We learned about Scrum process in brief, along with the different roles, events, and artifacts for the Scrum process. We will be covering different Agile concepts along the way while using the tooling system to meet the Agile team requirements.

We have GreenHopper installed and ready to use. We covered the basic terminology of GreenHopper, which we will be using further in this book. In the upcoming chapters, we will use this terminology and will cover each one in detail.

We covered different uses and examples of the tool, and which teams can use GreenHopper based on the variations and the nature of the teams. In the upcoming chapters, we will also cover managing both Scrum and Kanban teams using GreenHopper. Backlog creation, running Sprints, and reporting will be covered in detail.

We also covered different rich features of the GreenHopper interface which will come in handy for our day-to-day work and will result in a team productivity increase. In later chapters, we will cover each of the GreenHopper rich interface features and different functionality in details while managing both the Scrum and Kanban teams.

As mentioned in the project example, in the subsequent chapters, we will create a Scrum board for a website development Scrum team. We will create a product backlog, Sprints, a task board, and different reporting charts for the Scrum team. For the site operations team, we will create a Kanban team to control work in progress and to use the task board efficiently.

2
Planning Your Sprints with GreenHopper

The project backlog is a list of work accumulated over a period that needs to be done or that is already done. GreenHopper allows you to maintain your backlog and gives you a clear view of items for which work still needs to be done. To work in the Scrum way, you adopt an incremental pattern of completing your work.

In this chapter, we will cover creating boards to manage your backlog, analyzing the project backlog, planning the backlog in an incremental way, and grooming the backlog over a period of time. Based on ranked backlog, we will be creating a Sprint backlog and starting a sprint. To achieve this, we will be covering the following GreenHopper functionalities:

- **Creating a Jira project** to store backlog items in different issues type forms.
- **Creating a board** to visualize the backlog to be able to plan, work, and report on the backlog.
- **Creating Epic** to be able to break the backlog into multiple top-level functionalities, referred to as Theme or Epic.
- **Creating Story** to be able to break an Epic/functionality into smaller pieces of functionality or user stories.
- **Creating technical tasks** to be able to break the Story into smaller technical tasks required to deliver the functionality.
- **Ranking the backlog** to prioritize the backlog items in the order of delivered business value.
- **Creating a Sprint** to be able to deliver the backlog in incremental or iterative way.

Creating a project

GreenHopper is built on top of the Jira application. If you are already working with Jira and already have a project backlog in place, you can directly start creating a board for the existing projects, which we will be covering in the next section.

To get started with using GreenHopper, click on the **Getting Started** selection under the **Agile** tab in the top navigation of Jira.

As shown in the preceding screenshot, you have presets available to choose from, based on well-suited processes your team is currently working on, as follows:

- **Scrum Board** is for Agile teams following Agile Scrum methodology delivering in time-boxed iterations. The board created will provide you with Scrum terminology available on the board mapping with typical Scrum terms like Sprint, user story, Story points, Burndown chart, and so on.

- **Kanban** is for teams working in a controlled work flow manner that limits concurrent work in progress in a continuous flow of work. It allows you to prioritize work and control the flow of work at each stage or status using different constraints.

- **DIY** is used if you already have a Jira project in place and you follow a hybrid Agile process. You can use existing Jira projects and filters to create your board.

We will take an example of a typical Scrum team in this chapter and will create a Scrum board for the team. Click on the **create a new project and board** link, as shown in the previous screenshot, to create a new project and a Scrum board.

As shown in the preceding screenshot, to create a new Jira project from GreenHopper, enter the following values:

- **Project Name**: It is the name of the Jira project.

- **Project Key**: It's a unique identifier as the key for the project. All issues for the project will be prefixed with this key.

- **Project Lead**: This is the person leading the team or project. Based on your Jira project permissions this person will be assigned all Project Lead permissions, for example, default assignee of the issues, and so on.

- **Workflow**: It allows us to select relevant workflow for the project.

   ◦ **GreenHopper Simplified Workflow**: It allows you to add status and columns to your board dynamically and is much more powerful and flexible.

   ◦ **JIRA Default Workflow**: It allows you to use Jira's default workflow.

Based on your project configurations, you would still be able to switch workflow later. Accepting the default **GreenHopper Simplified Workflow** and clicking on **Create**, results in the new project with a default simplified workflow and lands you on a new project Scrum Board in the **Plan** mode.

Creating a board

A board in GreenHopper is a place to display issues from single or multiple projects. If you already have created a board in the last section, you may skip down to the next *Plan mode* section.

You can create a board by clicking on **create a new Scrum board** link as shown in the first screenshot on the **Getting started** page:

As shown in the preceding screenshot, enter the following values for new board:

- **Board Name**: The name of the board. You will also be able to edit the name of the board later.

- **Projects**: Allows you to select a single project or multiple projects based on your team configurations. GreenHopper also allows you to create a board based on multiple Jira projects. Based on your team configurations, if you are using an individual Jira project for each team, you can still create a single board to visualize and manage multiple teams.

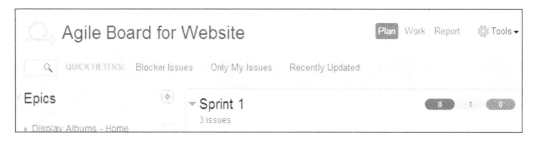

A typical Scrum board, displayed in the preceding screenshot, is the representation of three main phases; which are Planning, Tracking, and Reporting for an Agile project. On the right-hand side, the top panel represents the following modes.

Plan mode

Plan mode is used for planning your backlog items. You will be able to create a big functionality called Epic, displayed in left-side panel **Epics**. Create and add user stories for an Epic, and create technical tasks and subtasks for a Story. You will be able to rank different stories in backlog and estimate those stories based on Story points or business value.

 The **Plan** mode is only available in a Scrum board, not in a Kanban board, because you plan time-boxed delivery with Scrum and not in Kanban.

Work mode

Work mode allows the team to work on issues. Display different issues based on grouping multiple issues based on Story, priority, or other field values, even using complex and advanced JQL. You will be able to edit and change the status of issues in **Work** mode.

Report mode

Report mode helps you with sprint tracking and backlog reporting. You will be able to generate different reports based on a particular Sprint, Epic, cycle time, and so on for an issue.

To work efficiently with the board, you have instant search and quick filters available to you to find the right backlog items you want to work with.

To switch between different modes, click on **Plan**, **Work**, or **Report** link, as shown in following screenshot. To configure your board, click on **Configure** under **Tools** dropdown available in the right corner of the board.

Each board backlog item's selection is based on Jira filtering functionality. For a new board, it automatically creates a standard Jira filter to store filtering information. As shown in the following screenshot, select the **Filter** tab:

The following options display the selected Jira filter configurations for your board. Let us have a look at each of the options:

- **Saved Filter** is the filter which you can edit in Jira to change the issue selection settings for you.

- **Shares**: You can also edit share settings for your filter to share the board with the team.

- **Filter Query** is the JQL query generated using Jira filter criteria of issues.

- **Ranking** allows you to rank or order issues on the board. Make sure you enable ranking for your board to be able to prioritize your backlog items on the board.

To manage existing boards, click on the **Manage Boards** option under the **Agile** tab.

As shown in the preceding screenshot, it displays a list of all existing boards for your Jira instance. You can create a new board by using the **Copy** link with similar configurations, update the configuration for a board using the **Configure** link, and you can also delete an existing board by clicking on the **Delete** link.

To cancel the board configuration mode, click on the board title in the control bar.

Creating an Epic

An Epic is a large functionality of a product which needs to be delivered and which can further be divided into user stories. An Epic can span over multiple Sprints, until it is all finished.

As shown in the following screenshot, click on the **+** icon in the **Epics** panel to create an Epic:

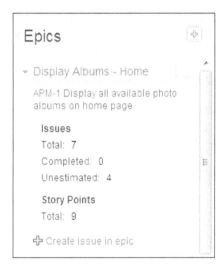

Create an Epic using the Epic issue type and enter the relevant details for your Epic. In the **Epics** panel, the **Epic name** you entered while creating the Epic is displayed along with issue details representing the Epic.

The panel also displays total issues (Story, improvements, bugs, and so on) assigned to an Epic along with the total estimates (here, Story points in our case for the Epic). For Epics created with no Epic name or missing Epic name, **unlabelled Epic** text is displayed.

Use drag-and-drop functionality on the **Epics** panel to rank the Epic within your backlog. Keep the high-priority Epic, which you will be working on first, on top.

To edit an Epic name, click on **Edit name**, which allows inline editing, as shown in the following screenshot:

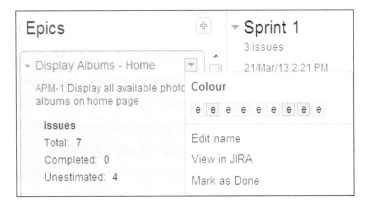

You can also distinguish an Epic with specific colors, and the corresponding Epic name will always be highlighted with that color in view.

Creating a Story

A user Story in Scrum is a user/actor conversation/requirement or a small functionality which can easily be unit tested and delivered in a limited time of a single Sprint. The Story belongs to an Epic.

To create a Story for an Epic, click on the **create issue in epic** link on **Epics** panel.

As shown in the preceding screenshot, to create a Story, select the relevant issue type and enter Story details. The newly created Story will be listed under an Epic and will also be visible in the **Plan** mode. If you select an Epic in the **Epics** panel, all the issues related to that Epic will be displayed on backlog panel. If you select one of the newly created stories, the Story panel is displayed on the right-hand side.

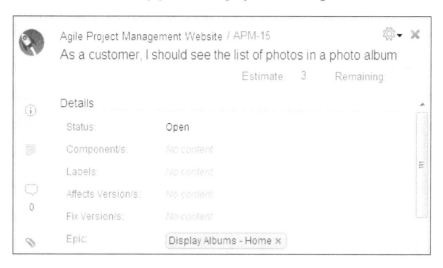

As shown in the preceding screenshot, the issue details panel is opened. You can perform all the relevant operations available to the issue on the same panel. The tag panel on the left-hand side allows you to do corresponding operations on the selected Story.

The Story details panel helps you with inline editing to edit the Story and related details. Using the **Actions** panel, you can edit and perform multiple operations related to Story.

Creating subtasks

The technical tasks are deliverable tasks performed by the developers to deliver a Story in a Sprint.

To add subtasks to a Story in the **Plan** mode, select a Story to add subtasks to, and the details panel of the Story will be visible.

As shown in the preceding screenshot, click on the **Create Sub-Task** button on the issue details panel to add a subtask to an issue. The same panel also displays the list of existing subtasks for an issue. Based on time tracking enabled for the Jira system, you will be able to add hour estimations for the technical tasks. If time tracking is enabled, the Story details panel also displays the total efforts required for all the subtasks, as shown at the bottom in the previous screenshot.

Ranking the backlog

By now you have your backlog ready with most of the required Epics which are further divided into different user stories to be delivered.

One of the important tasks in managing and grooming backlog is the ranking or ordering of different backlog items. From a business value perspective, not all functionality is of the same business value. Some functionalities are *must have* and some are *good to have*, having less business value.

As stated in the earlier section, you can rank Epics by drag-and-drop in the Epics panel and Epics will be relatively ranked in the panel. You will be able to focus on the Epic in the backlog which you are currently working upon.

To rank Story and other issue types in the backlog list, drag-and-drop vertically in the list based on the priority.

As shown in the preceding screenshot, you should be able to drag-and-drop each issue to prioritize it relatively. You can select multiple items in the backlog list by using *Ctrl + Click* or *Shift + Click* to move in the list or also to assign to a Sprint.

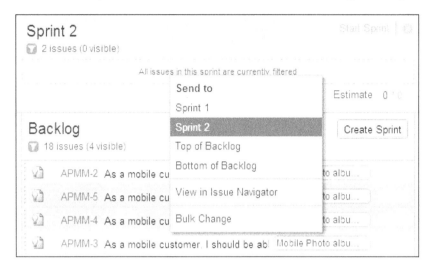

As shown in the preceding screenshot, you can do bulk operations on the selected issues. The following options are available:

- **Send to**: It is used to move multiple items to a selected Sprint during the Sprint planning event

- **Top of Backlog**: It is used to bulk prioritize the selected items by moving to the top of the backlog with highest ranking

- **Bottom of Backlog**: It is used to bulk prioritize the selected items by moving to the bottom of the backlog with lowest ranking

- **View in Issue Navigator**: It is used to view the selected items in Jira issue navigator

- **Bulk Change**: It's the functionality to bulk change the selected items, which can be editing issue details

You can also rank the technical tasks in the **Work** mode to move items based on priority, and teams can accordingly work on technical tasks based on pre-set priority.

Creating a Sprint

A Sprint in Scrum is an iteration to deliver a committed set of functionality for a product in a time box of nearly a month or less.

We have our prioritized backlog ready with us in the proper prioritized order. The next step is to estimate and pick a set of backlog items from product backlog to deliver in a particular Sprint. We will be covering the Sprint estimation process and capacity management in detail in the next chapter.

To create a Sprint, click on the **Create Sprint** button in the **Plan** mode under **Backlog** panel, as shown in the following screenshot:

It will create a blank Sprint for you. Click on the Sprint name to edit it with inline editing as per your current Sprint number. To plan the Sprint, click on the date fields for inline editing to set start and end dates for a Sprint.

To add Story items to a Sprint, drag stories based on preset ranking order of Story and drop it in the Sprint panel, the Sprint you are currently planning.

You can also select multiple items from the backlog panel, right-click, and send those to the newly created Sprint.

To start a Sprint, click on the **Start Sprint** link on the Sprint panel header in **Plan** mode, as shown in the following screenshot:

If you haven't set the Sprint timelines yet, once you start a Sprint, the start date and end date for the Sprint will be asked for in a Sprint start popup. The Sprint start and end date values will be referenced as the Sprint timelines to generate different reports like Burndown chart in the report panel. Starting the Sprint will move you from the **Plan** mode to the **Work** mode in the current board.

You can have only one Sprint as an active Sprint. For a single board, currently you can have only one Sprint as running or as an active Sprint. You can still create multiple Sprints in the **Plan** mode and those will still be inactive Sprints (you can't start working on those Sprints).

One of the practical scenarios for different projects is running multiple teams, and some teams do work on the same project backlog but also create team backlog out of a big project backlog. To achieve this, you can use multiple ways to create a team backlog, as well as multiple boards for multiple Sprints to run multiple teams.

For example, you can use **Labels field**, **Component field**, or **Custom field** to store team information. Take an example to run following teams, Orange, Green, and Blue.

As shown in the preceding screenshot, you can create multiple team boards designated specifically for each team. For example, **Team Blue Scrum Board**, **Team Green Scrum Board**, and **Team Orange Scrum Board** are displayed in the screenshot.

You will be able to start separate Sprints for each team working on team backlog which is part of the project backlog. You can update each backlog item to team backlog during Sprint planning only, so that same backlog item is not available to other teams.

Different teams use different approaches to use Jira, and GreenHopper's customizable and flexible nature helps teams to achieve what suits best to their requirements.

One additional feature of working with boards to access a GreenHopper view of items and a Jira view is the interchangeable nature. You can access your backlog items from boards directly in the issue navigator in Jira. There are multiple selection options available to switch to an issue navigator from the GreenHopper view. In a similar way, while browsing an issue in Jira, you can also switch to the GreenHopper view.

As shown in the preceding screenshot, the **Issues in Epic** panel and **Agile** panel in Jira view are displayed for an Epic issue type.

The issues in Epic panel lists down all the issues associated to the Epic in view. Agile panel option **View on Board** allows you to select a board that issue is listed in GreenHopper, and you can easily switch to your board view.

Summary

In this chapter, we created the team Agile board to get it started with Scrum way of working. We started the Agile team with a new Jira project and also with the existing project.

The board displayed the backlog items which the team will be working on. The team created different types of backlog items on the **Plan** mode. We created Epic and Story issues as part of the product backlog. We also covered creation of technical task items as part of Sprint planning meeting.

We also moved the items in the **Plan** mode to rank the items based on business prioritization. We will be covering the backlog items estimations in detail in the next chapter, where the team will learn to assign complexity points to each backlog item as part of backlog grooming and estimating.

Using **Plan** mode, the team created Sprint and committed on backlog items to be completed in a Sprint. The team started a Sprint and set the Sprint timelines to continue the Sprint. In later chapters, we will cover how to track a Sprint, working with the task board, and completing a Sprint in detail.

Estimating and Time Tracking

Every Agile team is different from each other and every team has its own way of working. Every team has its boundaries, capabilities, and smells. A team also evolves and adopts over a period of time to work together to deliver maximum value. Agile-based concepts are also built with the same mindset. We first need to know the team capabilities and rhythm over a period of time to fully understand the delivered value. In Scrum we call it the velocity of the team to deliver value in a Sprint. Based on the velocity of the team, we do the capacity planning as to how much a team can deliver in a Sprint and accordingly, plan the product and Sprint backlog.

In this chapter, we will cover the following to understand the estimating process, capacity planning, and time tracking better:

- Understanding the Estimating process
- Understanding Time tracking
- Using Story points to estimate story in GreenHopper
- Using ideal hours to estimate story in GreenHopper
- Using Business value to estimate story in GreenHopper
- Using hours for tracking in GreenHopper
- Using Tempo plugin for team and personal time tracking

Before we start with GreenHopper, we need to understand the idea behind estimating and capacity planning and the difference between estimating and tracking.

Estimating

Planning is a very critical part of any successful project delivery. One major concern with earlier software methodologies was the upfront planning and the team commitment even before starting the project. There are so many uncertainties possible which could not have been included upfront and the initial estimates could not precisely accommodate all of those. The initial estimates are in a way enforced on the team in the form of commitment even before starting the project.

Agile approach to the process of estimating and planning tries to target the same issue. Keeping Agile values in mind, the team and product owner work together in estimating and planning to deliver the maximum value. Both team and business work together in inspect and adapt mode.

One main point to understand here is that an Agile team measures the estimate in size rather than the duration. **Agile Estimating** is about measuring the chunk of work or functionality in relative terms.

The estimation size for different Agile teams varies, for Scrum it is called **Story Points**, a number assigned to a Story. Usually a team picks the smallest Story and assigns a number to it, and the Story is referred to as the **base Story**. In order to estimate another Story, the team compares the complexity of that Story with the base Story and gives it a relative number. Few teams use ideal days as an estimate size, but not based on the clock time. For other teams, it is business value for a Story, a number representing the value.

The issue with using actual elapsed clock hours, not the ideal days, is the uncertainty in the productive hours in current environment. Some of the typical activities a team member does in today's environment are as follows:

- **Meetings**: It includes scrum events, clarifications with product owner, design discussions, and so on
- **E-mail**: It includes clarifications and other e-mails
- **Multitasking**: It includes task switching and small discussions
- **Absence**: It includes planned Off, sick leave, holidays, and so on
- **Distractions**: It includes phone calls, small discussions, and so on

The productive time for a team member is not same as the clock time for a work day. You can put a buffer around the actual productive hours in estimating, but the approach should be to pick the right one between planning the working and work the plan. The suggested approach is to analyze the nonproductive hours using tracking, and improve upon it, rather than estimating the Story in actual hours.

In addition to the business stories, consider adding and sizing technical-facing stories to rank track along with features. Technical-facing stories can include spike for researching a change in tools, architecture restructuring, refactoring legacy code for maintainability, and so on.

Time tracking

Time tracking is to understand how the team is spending time or how much effort in hours a particular technical task or subtask will take. Each Story is further broken down into technical tasks for which we can assign hours in estimations. Each technical task is picked up by a team member and hours are logged for that task.

The time tracking effort at the task level gives us further insight on how much effort in hours has already been spent on the task and how much effort is still required. The actual work hours logged in the system can further help to improve on reducing the non-productive hours for the team.

Estimating using GreenHopper

GreenHopper provides you the following options for estimating your backlog items:

Story points

Story points are relative numbers assigned to a Story representing the Story complexity in comparison to base Story. The velocity will be calculated based on the Story points covered in a Sprint. If no time tracking is selected, the Burndown chart will display the number of Story points completed over Sprint timelines.

Original time estimate

Original time estimates are the ideal days or hours that will be used for the estimations. The team velocity will be measured in hours.

Business value

Business value refers to the business value delivered by an issue. Further data will also be calculated against the business value field data.

Issue count

The issue count is the number of issues planned for a sprint. Here, no estimations would be required. The velocity will also be calculated based on the total number of issues delivered in a sprint. To configure the estimation statistics, as to which field will be used for estimations, navigate to your team board and click on **Configure** under the **Tools** options.

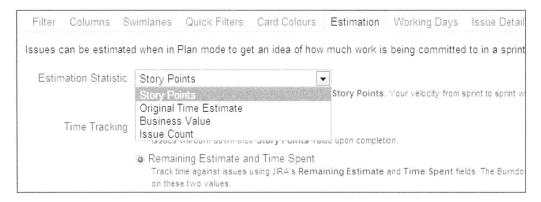

As shown in the preceding screenshot, you can configure **Estimation Statistics** and **Time Tracking** options in the configuration screen.

To enable the tracking, under the same **Estimation** tab, select the **Remaining Estimate and Time Spent** radio choice which will use the Jira time tracking fields.

Estimating the backlog with Story points

Story points are the estimate size representing the size of a Story. All we need to know about a Story is whether it is a small Story or large Story. The Story points are relative numbers that different teams use for different strategies. The idea is to pick a small user Story covering the most portion of layers of the product or application and assign a number to it. For the rest of the stories, compare those with this Story and assign a relative number in terms of size.

We will see how we can estimate a Story with Story points in GreenHopper. Navigate to the board configuration screen, under **Estimation** tab configure the **Estimation Statistics**, and select the **Story Points** option as shown in the previous screenshot.

You can add Story points to a Story while creating the Story itself, as shown in the following screenshot.

The **Story Points** field is available to issue the types, Story and Epic by default. Update the custom field configurations in Jira to add it to other issue types. If you want to add Story points to your bugs, improvement, and so on, you need to update the Jira field and screen configurations accordingly.

Usually the stories, backlog items are already in place while doing the estimation and planning the meeting. Click on **Story**, and edit the **Estimate** value in Story details panel as shown in the following screenshot:

As shown in the preceding screenshot, you can use the inline editing functionality to update estimates for the Story.

As soon as you update the estimates for a Story, the relevant panels of backlog items and epic also get updated. The Sprint backlog gets updated as shown in following screenshot:

In case no time tracking is selected for estimation, the burndown chart shows the number of Story points completed over a period of time.

The velocity for the Sprint is measured in the Story points completed by the team in the Sprint.

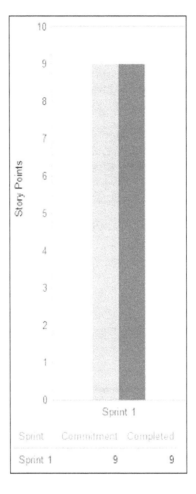

In the preceding screenshot, the committed and completed Story points for initial Sprint are shown. Over a period of time, the team figures out the velocity and Story points delivered in a Sprint in an accurate way.

From a capacity planning perspective, the team commits on the number of Story points delivered as per the velocity of the team.

Estimating the backlog with hours

You can also use ideal days, as explained in earlier sections, to estimate your backlog item.

Go to your team board configuration screen, and under the **Estimation** tab configure the **Estimation Statistics**, and select the **Original Time Estimate** option.

The **Original Estimate** field is used to store hour information for estimations. To add an estimate, update the field value with original estimates while creating an issue.

As shown in the preceding screenshot, you will be using Jira time tracking functionality and corresponding fields. You can use the same Jira time tracking format to enter the estimates.

You can also use the issue details page to update the estimates. The **Estimate** field value is automatically updated for the original estimate time field.

As shown in the preceding screenshot, you can enter hour estimates in the Jira time format. The hour estimation values are automatically updated in the backlog items panel and accordingly epic details are also updated in the view.

The Burndown chart shows the completion of original estimates on issue completion.

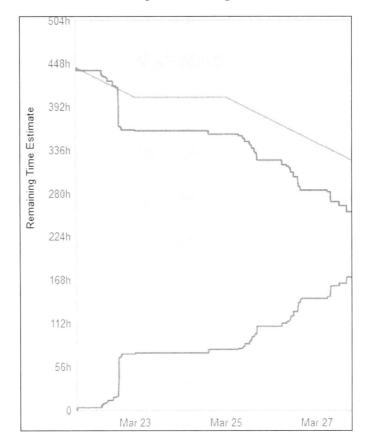

As shown in the preceding screenshot, the Burndown chart is displayed to represent the work that is remaining and completed, in hours over the Sprint timelines. The velocity for Sprint is also measured in hours.

Estimating the backlog with business value

Business value is a custom field which allows measurement of an issue based on the business value delivered by the issue. It allows you to add your team specific measurement values in number format for an issue.

Go to your team board configuration screen, under **Estimation** tab configure the **Estimation Statistics**, and select **Business Value** option.

To add the business value estimates, update the **Business Value** field in the issue create screen, as shown in the following screenshot:

The burndown chart data is displayed based on the completion of business value over period of time. The velocity of the team is measured in terms of total business value delivered in a Sprint.

Estimating the backlog with issue count

Issue count represents the total number of issues completed in a Sprint. There is no estimation required here. GreenHopper automatically generates the information for you.

The burndown chart displays the completion of count of issue over a period time in a Sprint. The velocity is measured in total issues completed in a Sprint.

Time tracking with hours

As explained in earlier section, GreenHopper allows you to select time tracking and accordingly the burndown chart information is displayed to you.

Go to your team board configuration screen, under **Estimation** tab configure the **Time Tracking** option, and select the **Remaining Estimate and Time Spent** option as shown in the following screenshot:

The time tracking information is available based on the **Remaining Estimate and Time Spent** field.

The original estimates for the technical tasks are added once the team creates the tasks for a Story. As the team works on the technical tasks, the hours are logged into the system against the technical tasks.

As shown in the preceding screenshot, based on logged work, the remaining time and time spent for the technical tasks is updated. The burndown chart will also display the updated data based on hours data updates.

Time tracking with Tempo plugin

Tempo is a time tracking Jira plugin. It is quite helpful in both planning and time tracking for your team.

 Tempo is a commercial plugin and checks the trial version for evaluation.

Some of the important features of the plugin are:

- The ability to log work easily and quickly
- Clear visual indicators
- Inline editing

- The ability to manage internal meeting
- Vacation planning
- Timesheet generation
- The ability to map people, teams, and projects
- Easy and nice integration with GreenHopper
- The ability to export data to Excel

As shown in the preceding screenshot, you can generate reports at individual, team, and project levels for timesheet purposes. We can take full advantage of both estimating and time tracking to plan the Sprint in a much better way now.

Summary

We covered the difference between estimating and time tracking for your agile team. We estimated backlog items based on different measurement units available with GreenHopper. We estimated the stories in terms of Story points for relative size and complexity. In upcoming chapters we will see how the estimation values can be tracked using the Burndown chart in reporting functionality.

We covered the time tracking for technical tasks. We entered original estimates in hours for the technical tasks during Sprint planning. We covered the Jira add-on Tempo plugin to help us in capacity management and timesheet reporting purpose. We learned to use an easy and advanced time tracking plugin to improve upon nonproductive time and to handle uncertainties.

In upcoming chapters we will cover how to use the task board for day-to-day technical tasks for the team. Teams will be able to pick the technical tasks and log hours on tasks. We will cover the charts to display the hour efforts information used for tracking and reporting.

4
Using the Work Board to Update Issues

Agile process is about people, team, interactions, collaboration, sharing, learning, and continuous improvement. And the task board for an agile team is the heart of it. Task boards are the information radiators for day-to-day tasks for a developer.

In this chapter, we will cover the following to understand how to create and work with task boards using GreenHopper suiting your needs best:

- Understanding the task board
- Scrum default task boards in GreenHopper
- Using GreenHopper Simplified Workflow
- Adding a column to the task board
- Updating issue status on the task board
- Viewing issue details on the task board
- Updating issue details on the task board
- Using keyboard shortcuts on the task board
- Ranking issues on the task board

Understanding the task board

Before we start using a task board, let's understand the uses and importance of a task board and what makes a great task board.

A task board represents the visual information of work in progress. It shows how much work still needs to be done, how much work is in progress, and how much work has already been completed. Every Scrum team day starts with the daily standup status in front of the task board, covering basic questions of how much work each team member has finished since the last meeting, and what work will be in progress till the next meeting, and if there are any impediments.

To answer the question of what makes a task board a great one, we need to understand a typical day in a developer's life, the team dynamics, and a bit of high level view from project a and organization perspective. Some of the requirements from a task board which differs from one to another are:

- Alignment to the development process
- Prioritized backlog of Story and technical tasks
- Must be easy to read and visualize
- Must be easy to update a task status
- Single view or status to team and all stakeholders
- Clear visualization of impediments or flagged issues
- Display up-to-date information
- Clear display of big size tasks, break into smaller ones
- Color combination to highlight the nature of task
- Flexibility to add work flow columns
- Team calendar to display each member availability for the Sprint
- Ability for tracking information along with estimates

Many more such additional benefits can be made available if we think of digital versions of such task boards, which cater to the further requirements of a distributed team, team collaboration, and cooperation.

Scrum task board in GreenHopper

A typical Scrum board consists of three status for the work planned in a Sprint:

- **To Do**: The work that still needs to be done in a Sprint
- **In Progress**: The work that is in progress and a team member is currently working on the same
- **Done**: The work already done for the task and it is marked as completed

As covered in earlier chapters, you already have created a Scrum board for your team. You are also ready with the prioritized Sprint backlog and have started a Sprint. The next step is to visualize the same Sprint backlog information on the task board so that team members can start working on it.

To access the task board, go to your team board and click on the **Work** link. The default Scrum board in GreenHopper has three columns representing the status of work as shown in the following screenshot:

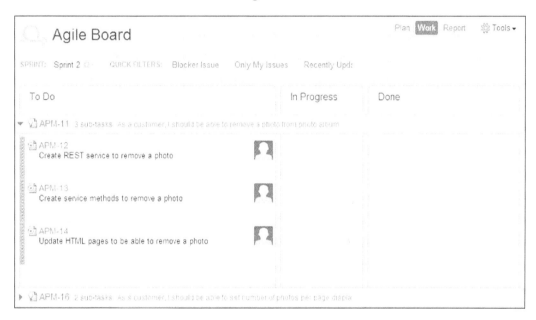

Once you start a Sprint, all the issues are into the do state and the team still need to start working on the issues.

Using GreenHopper Simplified Workflow

Workflows control the transition between the different statuses of an issue. If you create your project using Jira project creation flow, the default Jira workflow will be assigned to your issues. If you create your project and board using the **Getting Started** page under GreenHopper, you can choose to use **GreenHopper Simplified Workflow**.

The main difference between Jira workflow and simplified workflow is that simplified workflow allows free transition of issues between statuses where Jira workflow has a condition that can be configured. On status transition, no screens are displayed for the simplified workflow, it is an instant transition. For Jira workflow, you may have additional status transition screens. Simplified workflow can only be modified in GreenHopper mode.

To check your board workflow settings, navigate to the **Tools** action, click on the **Configure** option and select the **Columns** tab.

Notice the **Simplified Workflow** option, displaying **Using GreenHopper Simplified Workflow** which allows us to add an additional status on the fly.

Click on the **Add Status** button to add a status for the issues.

As shown in the preceding screenshot, enter the name of the status as `Verify`. We need to create a column on the task board to track all the issues which needs to be verified and having status as **Verify**.

If you are using the Jira default workflow scheme, GreenHopper allows you to switch to **GreenHopper Simplified Workflow**. As shown in the following screenshot, click on the button **Simplify workflow** and your workflow will be switched, and you will be able to add a status on the fly.

In case the **Simplified Workflow** shows a message **GreenHopper Simplified Workflow unavailable**, check your project workflow configurations or contact the product support team.

Adding a column to the task board

In actual projects, the workflow of the issues is still quite complex. The team starts working on an issue, completes the development, deploys it to Quality Assurance environment, sends it for user acceptance testing, and a few more intermediate steps, then it can be marked as completed. We need additional columns and status for the task board and issues for this.

Go to the **Tools** action, click on the **Configure** option and select the **Columns** tab.

The following screenshot displays the default status for the issues and the default columns for a Scrum task board based on Jira default configurations.

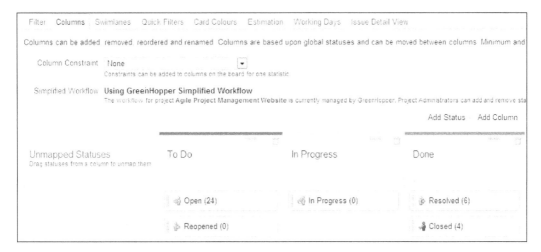

Click on the **Add Column** button to add a column to the task board.

Enter the name of the column as Verify. If you only have one unmapped status, **Verify** in our case, it will automatically be mapped to a new column. Otherwise drag and drop the **Verify** status from the **Unmapped Status** column to the newly added **Verify** column.

Go to your team board and click on the **Work** link, your newly added column **Verify** will be added to the task board as shown in the following screenshot.

The new column **Verify** will display all the issues with the newly created status `Verify`. As soon as developers finish progress on the task, it can further be moved to testing team to verify the same.

Updating an issue status on the task board

Each column on the task board represents a single or multiple status. GreenHopper allows drag-and-drop functionality to update issue status. Based on your workflow selection, you can move an issue around different statuses on the task board.

As in the preceding example, transition between different statuses is possible. You can mark an issue from the **Verify** state to the **To Do** state with a possible status option of **Open** or **Reopened**.

While drag-and-drop in case of possibility of multiple statuses for a column, you can select to one of the available statuses. The color visualization of different issue statuses while dragging makes it much easier to update the status on the task board.

As shown in following screenshot, you can move this particular issue either to an **Open** state or a **Reopened** state based on your requirements:

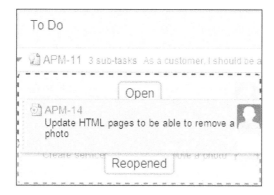

You can also update an issue status in Jira view and the status will automatically be updated on the task board.

Updating issue details on the task board

While working on an issue, the team needs to update issue details. There can be multiple operations which can be required for a task as follows:

- Assign issue to myself or a team member
- Edit issue details such as the summary or description
- Log work on the issue
- Display quick details about Story to which the issue belongs to
- View comments on the issue
- View attached files to the issue

You would be able to do all the preceding and many more operations related to a task being on the task board itself. All these actions can be performed in the issue details panel.

To view an issue detail, click on the issue key link on the task board. The issue details panel will be displayed as shown in following screenshot on the right-hand side of the board displaying the details for the selected issue:

The tag panel allows you to view issue details, description, comments, and files attached to the issue.

The inline editing functionality will allow you to update issue details. The action dropdown will allow you to do different operations on that issue such as assigning, log work, workflow action, and so on as available in the Jira view.

The resolved issues are displayed as striked out on the task board.

Using keyboard shortcuts on the task board

Jira keyboard shortcuts are a nice functionality to work with issues in an efficient way. There are global keyboard shortcuts and also Agile shortcuts which can be used on the task board. Some of the very useful keyboard shortcuts are listed as follows:

- **Project Mode**: Use the letter *Z* on the keyboard for full board view that hides top navigation clutter.

- **Next Issue**: Use the letter *J* on the keyboard to move to the next issue downwards in a column

- **Previous Issue**: Use the letter *K* on the keyboard to move to the previous issue upwards in a column

- **Next Column**: Use the letter *N* on the keyboard, to move to the top item in the next column.

- **Previous Column**: Use the letter *P* on the keyboard, to move to the topmost item in the previous column.

- **Toggle Details View**: Use the letter *T* on the keyboard, to show and hide details view of selected issues on the task board.

- **Assign to Me**: Use the letter *I* on the keyboard, to assign a selected issue to yourself on the task board.

- **Edit Issue**: Use the letter *E* on the keyboard, to edit and issue on the task board.

- **Log Work**: Use the dot (.) on the keyboard to open the operations dialog, and select **action Log Work** to open the Log work dialog window.

- **Toggle Swimlane**: Use the dash (-) on the keyboard to toggle between expand and collapse of the swimlanes on the task board.

To access the full list of keyboard shortcuts, press *?* on your keyboard. Make sure you currently don't have cursor location in a text field, otherwise press *Esc* first.

Ranking issues on the task board

We have already prioritized the Sprint backlog ready with the team to start working upon. The team has the list of technical tasks on the task board which needs to be worked upon.

Each Story has a list of technical tasks attached to it. Most commonly the Scrum teams take the approach of pulling work from the **To Do** list rather than the Scrum master pushing it to the team. Each team member picks up a task from the list of ranked tasks on the task board. Based on inter-dependency of technical tasks, a decision needs to be made if it can be divided among multiple team members or if it would be easier if a single developer picks up similar tasks. This is up to the team dynamics considering what fits the team best.

GreenHopper allows us to rank tasks on the task board. As shown in the following screenshot, use drag-and-drop functionality to rank the tasks on the task board in a column. Make sure that ranking is enabled in the board used filter to be able to rank issues.

One remaining feature of the task board is using **Swimlane** to group similar issues together and using quick filters to work efficiently. We will be covering this feature in detail in the later chapters.

Summary

We are now familiar with the Scrum task board and importance of the task board for the team. We covered the default Scrum task board provided by GreenHopper.

We covered using GreenHopper Simplified Workflow to add new status and new column to our task board which can further be configured based on team-specific requirements.

We covered further how to view items on the task board and to update issue status and details on the task board itself. In the upcoming chapter, we will be covering how we can use Quick filter functionality to filter only the relevant issues on the task board.

We used GreenHopper drag-and-drop functionality to rank tasks on the task board itself to divide it better among the team members. We covered some common keyboard shortcuts to help us to work efficiently with Jira and GreenHopper.

In the next chapter, we will be covering the horizontal grouping functionality, Swimlane, and how to group issues on task group.

5
Using Quick Filters and Highlighting Issues

Most of the large enterprise projects span over months, and even years. Each one of these will have projects has some large backlogs to handle. Maintaining such large backlog, filtering necessary data, and visualizing the relevant information are very important aspects of any backlog management tool.

In this chapter, we will cover functionality to filter on backlog items and to visualize the relevant information accordingly. This chapter will include the following:

- Working with filters for project backlog
- Working with Quick Filters
- Working with Swimlane
- Using card colors

Working with filters for project backlog

Each board created with GreenHopper automatically creates a Jira filter for you. This filter contains the backlog item's listing criteria. To view the configured filter for your board, go to your team board. Open the **Tools** action, click on **Configure**, and select the **Filter** tab.

As shown in the preceding screenshot, the following filter information is available:

- **Saved Filter**: The Jira filter containing the backlog item's selection criteria.
- **Shares**: With whom all the board items will be shared is configured via filter sharing permissions.
- **Filter Query**: The JQL query used in the selected filter as selection criteria.
- **Ranking**: Allows ordered ranking of issues on the **Plan** mode.

Each project has large backlog items, ideally at a particular moment you only work on part of the large backlog items. Jira filtering capability allows you to filter on your backlog using different filtering criteria. To edit filters in Jira, click on the **View in Issue Navigator** link, as shown in the preceding screenshot.

The filter information is displayed in the issue navigator. You can use Jira's simple or advanced options to update the filter configurations. As shown in the following screenshot, the filter is displayed in the issue navigator view:

Either you can use basic filter criteria based on standard fields or you can also use advanced search using JQL to extend your filtering.

Working with Quick Filters

GreenHopper provides additional functionality called **Quick Filters** to filter on items currently displayed on the **Plan** and **Work** mode. Quick Filters are additional JQL conditions applied on the displayed items.

Take an example of multiple teams for a project where you have a design team, frontend team, and backend team working together to deliver the functionality. Based on your issue's screen configurations, you have additional fields where, for each technical task, you assign a resource type to represent which team it belongs to. As shown in the following screenshot, you can further divide your items based on available team resource selection:

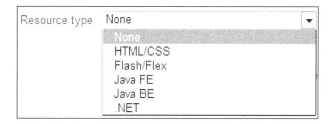

We will be creating a few Quick Filters to be able to filter on backlog specific to each team. To access Quick Filters configuration for your board, open the **Tools** action, click on **Configure**, and go to the **Quick Filters** tab.

As shown in the preceding screenshot, to add a Quick Filter, enter name of the filter and JQL query for your filter, and click on the **Add** button. Use inline editing to edit an existing Quick Filter name or query. To remove any of existing filters, click on the **Delete** button.

For the previous example, we have created three new Quick Filters for three different teams based on the **Resource type** field value.

The Quick Filter is displayed on your board's **Plan** and **Work** mode. As shown in the following screenshot, you have additional filtering options for the **Design Team**, **Frontend Team**, and **Backend Team** items.

Once you select one of the Quick Filters, the corresponding JQL condition is applied to your displayed backlog items. If you are in the **Plan** mode, the product backlog items will be filtered based on the selected Quick Filter's additional JQL. If you are on **Work** mode, the task board items will be applied based on selected Quick Filter additional JQL condition.

Selecting more than one Quick Filter combines the JQL query conditions that filter the issues visible in the board.

Working with Swimlane

For various Agile teams, grouping issues together based on parent task or other matching criteria is very important. For example, grouping all technical tasks belonging to a story is quite common. But each team has its unique issue data, workflow conditions, and prioritization behavior.

While working on the work/task board, we have grouped or categorized the issues together in a vertical way based on issue status. Each column groups issues having the same status or equal to statuses defined for the column.

To be able to group issues in a horizontal way, GreenHopper provides additional functionality of a **Swimlane**. A Swimlane is a categorization of issues in a horizontal way on task board.

To access Swimlane settings, open the **Tools** action under your team board and click on **Configure**. Then, go to the **Swimlanes** tab.

As shown in the preceding screenshot, you have the following options available to configure Swimlanes.

Queries

JQL query is used to define grouping of issues.

Select **Queries** from the drop-down list and create your board specific JQL which is relevant to your team.

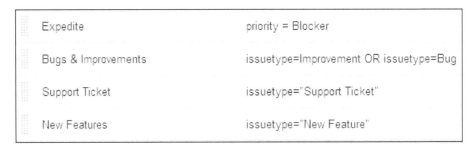

As shown in the previous screenshot, some of the Swimlanes are created based on issue type and priority.

To add/edit/delete a Swimlane, you can use the same configuration screen.

The configured Swimlanes will be visible on your work board. The board will display the horizontal categorization of issues under these lanes.

As shown in preceding screenshot, the Swimlanes are displayed on your task board grouping issues together that follow relevant JQL criteria.

The Swimlanes only appear when issues matching their Query Filter are visible on the board and the Swimlanes appear in the order they were created in.

Stories

Usually for agile teams, the story acts as the parent issue, and a team wants to categorize all the technical tasks under parent story itself. Swimlane functionality supports that very well.

Select the **Stories** value in the drop-down to display each story as the Swimlane.

Assignees

You can display horizontal categorization for the issues based on the current assignee of the issues and select to show unassigned issues above or below the assigned issues.

No Swimlanes

No horizontal categorization will be applied on your work board with the **No Swimlanes** option.

Both vertical and horizontal grouping and categorization of issues gives you much more flexibility to maintain and visualize you current work backlog.

Highlighting issues

Highlighting issues on the board based on different properties and behavior is very important. Looking at issues, even without reading the issue details, gives you some hint as to what kind of issue is available. Additional visual effects make it much easier for the end user to work with the board.

Epics have a highlighting feature that we touched upon already. You can select specific colors for an Epic and all references of the epic name will be visible in that color.

As shown in the preceding screenshot, you can assign a specific color to an Epic. Highlighting an Epic makes it easier to work on the **Plan** mode, and it makes it easier to pick color stories on the board.

While working on **Work** mode, you can select specific card colors for your issues based on different settings or configurations.

To view your current card colors settings, open **Tools** action, click on **Configure**, and select **Card Colours** tab.

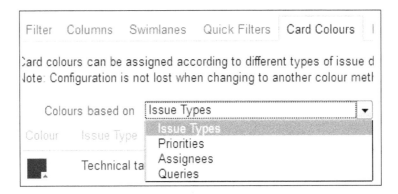

As shown in the preceding screenshot, we have the following options available to select the right selection of card display colors for your board.

Issue types

It's used to assign specific card color based on the issue type of the Jira issue. Depending on the variety of issues on your project, see if this combination will work for your team.

Some teams do have quite complex issue combinations within the same Jira project mapping requirements for different teams. You can use issue type card colors to differentiate between high priority Production Bug from regular Sprint Feature Bug belonging to a story.

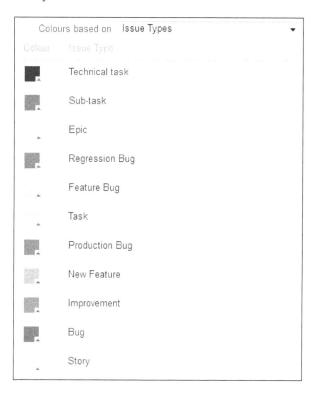

As shown in the preceding screenshot, you can assign your own team color to different cards based on the issue types. Changing these issue type colors only overrides the system default issue type colors as they appear on this board.

Priority

Priority allows using the issue's priority specific colors to visualize high or low priority issues differently. For example, you can use the red color to identify any of the blocker issues.

Assignees

Assignees allows using issue's current assignee to set the color for the issue. Each team member can assign a color and it would be easy for team members to visualize their own issues with the help of card colors.

Queries

Queries allow you to use a combination of above conditions and create your own JQL to assign a color to it. Each issue matching the JQL criteria will be assigned the corresponding color. For example, you can select the red color for the issues for which cycle time is high, which have not been updated since last n number of days.

Identifying issues on your board based on different colors makes it much easier to work with a large backlog of items.

Summary

We covered different ways to work with large backlog items covering backlog management from small to large scale projects. We learned to use Jira filtering functionality to work on limited product backlog for your team board.

We are now familiar with Quick Filters to quickly filter on issues on **Plan** and **Work** mode. Using Quick Filter functionality, you should be able to filter an entire backlog based on an advanced search of JQL matching your issue data.

We are now familiar with Swimlane functionality for grouping items on a task board horizontally to visualize and prioritize the work in much better way. Horizontal grouping allows you to manage backlog on task board in a much better and easier way for better productivity.

We also covered issues highlighting functionality to visually distinguish the relevant issue information in a quick and easy way.

In upcoming chapters, we will be covering how to use GreenHopper reporting functionality for sprint tracking and project reporting using different charts.

6
Understanding the Burndown Chart

Two of the important aspects of Agility are visibility and simplicity. Every Agile team believes in visibility of work progress, communication, and collaboration. In earlier times, we used to have quite complex metrics around to track team progress. In Agile, to track team progress in a particular Sprint, we use quite a simple chart called **Burndown chart** to represent how much work is remaining and how much has been done over the time of Sprint.

In this chapter, we will be covering the following things:

- The Burndown chart
- Typical Burndown charts
- Viewing Burndown charts in GreenHopper
- Burndown chart measurement units
- Configuring working and non-working days
- Scope management for a Sprint

Burndown chart

The Burndown chart is a graphical representation of work left over a period of time for a particular Sprint. The y axis in the chart contains the work left in team measurement units which can vary from team to team, and the x axis is the time in days. The following screenshot shows you a Burndown chart sample:

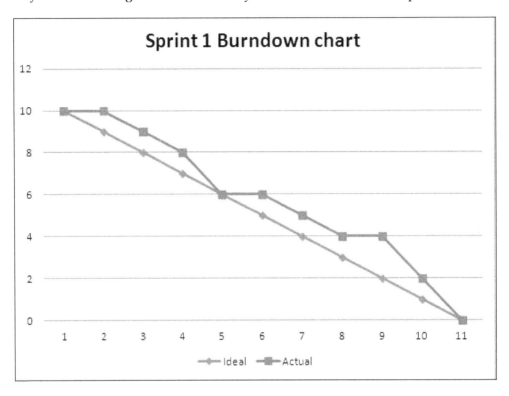

The y axis represents the measurement units of work which can be Story points, business value, or hours. The x axis in the chart represents the Sprint timeline in days.

During the start of the Sprint, all the work is in the "to do" state. As the Sprint progresses, the tasks are completed and the work remaining decreases over time. The **Ideal** graph is a guideline representing the ideal burn over time. The **Actual** graph represents the work burn over time by the team.

Typical Burndown charts

The Ideal Burndown chart, in the preceding diagram, represents how work should be completed over time in a Sprint by the team. But in practical scenarios, the estimated values don't work in linear ways. There are days when more productivity is achieved and there are days when the curve may be stagnant.

Your team Burndown chart will also show the team state, as to whether the team is working at a sustainable pace or not. Use the Burndown chart throughout the Sprint to gauge progress and take corrective action when necessary, and also as a historic guide for planning the next Sprint commitments.

We will first discuss some typical Burndown charts which will give you some understanding about how a team is performing in a particular Sprint. The charts won't picture the actual nature and scenario for a team, but it is just an indication you can get from the chart.

Ideal team

The team burns the Sprint backlog as close to the linear way as possible.
The estimated work is burned in an ideal way and the team is able to complete the Sprint. It is hard to achieve a linear work burn but every team tries to and works towards achieving close to the Ideal graph.

Good or great team

The team knows the velocity, the work burn chart may not be linear, but the team delivers the Sprint easily. The initial flat nature of the curve usually represents the preparation work for the Sprint and the work in progress, but in the end, the remaining work comes close to Ideal as the team reaches completion. The team works on estimation and backlog grooming to adapt to better linear burn nature of work.

Overloaded team

This team is the team that has committed to do more work than it could finish. The curve for actual work is always above the ideal work burn curve. In the end, the remaining work is never finished and team is not able to meet Sprint goals.

Not enough work

In this, the team completes the Sprint much earlier and doesn't have enough work to pick an extra Story, and the Sprint got completed earlier. The quick decline in the remaining work below the Ideal graph and the team very easily meets the Sprint goals before time.

Less work committed

The actual work burn curve is also below your ideal work burn curve which means that the team committed to less work than they could deliver.

Scope change

Here, the team agreed to deliver some work, but during the scope of the Sprint, additional work was added or some work was replaced, which is also clearly visible in the chart.

The Burndown chart for each team will vary, it is just an indication of how the team is burning work in a Sprint. Based on the different natures of the charts, you need to work with the team to analyze them further. Some of the typical features of the Burndown chart tool are:

- Display progress details for the Sprint
- Current and ideal progress details
- Show productivity bottlenecks in the progress
- Track team velocity
- Include the non-working days
- Ability to print the charts

Viewing the Burndown chart in GreenHopper

To view the Burndown chart, as shown in the following screenshot, go to the **Agile** tab, select your Agile team board, and click on the **Report** link and select **Burndown Chart**.

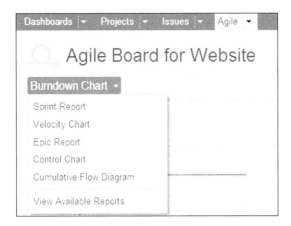

It will display the Burndown chart for your currently running Sprint. To see the Burndown chart for a Sprint, you need to start the Sprint first in the **Plan** mode.

You can view the Burndown chart for active Sprint. You can also see the chart for the completed Sprint.

As shown in the following screenshot, you can select to view the Burndown chart for finished Sprints and the currently active Sprint.

Looking at earlier Sprint Burndown charts, you can compare how the team is performing over releases in term of completing work in a Sprint. As discussed in the earlier section based on the nature of typical Burndown charts, you will be able to compare Burndown charts for different Sprints and take relevant next steps to improve upon how work is completed in a Sprint.

Burndown chart measurement units

The measurement criteria for Burndown charts depend on the estimation process you have selected earlier. To view the estimation statistics, click on the **Tools** action, select **Configure**, and go to the **Estimation** tab.

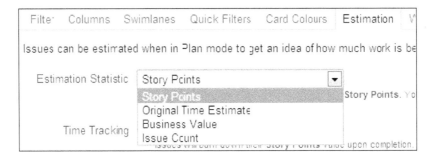

If time tracking is not enabled (which means the option **None** under **Time Tracking** is selected), the Burndown chart is based on the estimation statistics selected by you. As shown in the preceding screenshot, the following options are available to select the estimation statistics and accordingly, the Burndown chart value will be displayed:

- **Story Points**: Issues will burn Story points on completion of the issue.

- **Original Time Estimate**: The estimated efforts in hours, for the original estimate field will burn on completion of issue.

- **Business Value**: Issues will burn business value on completion of the issue.

- **Issue Count**: The number of issues remaining will burn on completion of the issue.

If time tracking is enabled, the **Remaining Time Estimate and Time Spent** value will be displayed for the Burndown chart.

Configuring working and non-working days

GreenHopper allows you to change the time zone settings for your board. You can also configure which weekdays your team will be working. You can also set which days your team will not be working based on holidays and vacations.

To set working and non-working days for your team, go to the **Tools** action, select **Configure**, and go to the **Working Days** tab. As shown in the following screenshot, you have the following configuration available to set the time zone, working, and non-working days for your team.

Time zone

The time zone allows you to select which time zone the team is working in.

Standard working days

You have to select each day of the week the team normally works. The days not selected will appear as a grey background in the Burndown chart, as shown in the following screenshot:

Non-working days

This allows you to configure the holidays on which teams won't be working. Click on the **Add Date** button to add a non-working date to the list.

As shown in the following screenshot, you will be able to choose to display non-working days on Burndown chart. The changes on the working days will be reflected in your Burndown chart.

You can choose whether or not to display non-working days on your Burndown chart. If selected, non-working days appear as a grey background in the Burndown chart.

Scope management for Sprint

In ideal cases, we assume that the scope for a Sprint is closed when we start a Sprint. The team commits at the start of a Sprint that they will be delivering in a Sprint. But, in many of the practical scenarios that does not work well.

Based on new insights and priority changes, the product owner asks to change a Story during the Sprint. Usually from the team side, if work on a particular Story is not started and a new Story is of equal size, then team agrees to switch the Story during the Sprint. Another scenario can be that you finish your work earlier and the team can pick some Story from the backlog. All the scope changes are reflected in the Burndown chart in terms of addition or removal of work from the Sprint backlog.

To remove a Story from a Sprint, as shown in the following screenshot, click on the Story issue key and the Story details panel will be displayed. Go to **Actions** and select **Remove from Sprint**. This option only appears in the Action menu for issue types (for example, Epics or Stories), and not subtasks.

The issue and associated subtasks will be removed from the Sprint. You can go to the **Plan** mode and add additional stories to the Sprint.

The changes in the scope of the Sprint are clearly displayed in the Burndown chart. Take the cursor on the change point in the Burndown chart which will display the details of the scope change at that point.

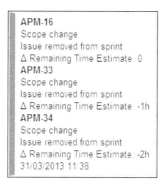

As shown in the previous screenshot, the scope change will be clearly visible, giving an indication to both the team and the product owner what has been added or removed during a Sprint.

The scope change in terms of remaining estimates and time spent is clearly visible in the below diagram which represents on a particular day how the scope changed for the team in terms of work in a Sprint.

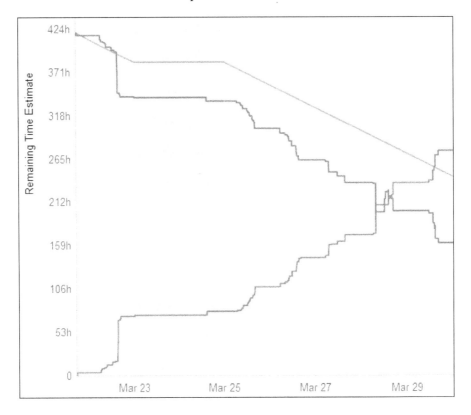

As shown in the preceding screenshot, the amount of remaining efforts in hours was changed because of addition of work or new insights during the Sprint. The dark grey line in the Burndown chart represents the guideline that illustrates the adjusted projection with the scope changes.

Summary

The Burndown chart is one of the major artifacts of the Scrum framework. Looking at the single chart can give you an indication of how much was planned, how teams are doing over a period of time in a Sprint, and whether teams will be able to achieve what they have committed to.

In this chapter, we covered the importance of the Burndown chart and some typical charts to compare your team state. In the next chapter, we'll cover how you would be able to state team status and progress looking at your team chart.

We also covered how to generate a Burndown chart in GreenHopper for your team. You can use Story points, ideal hours, or business value estimations to generate your Burndown chart.

In the upcoming chapters we will be covering to end a Sprint, generate Sprint report, and also finish an Epic. We will be able to generate different project reporting charts.

We also covered the scope change representation of work in the Burndown chart itself. You can also configure working and non-working days for your team to generate more relevant statistics in your chart.

7
Ending a Sprint

We have already covered backlog prioritization to get it ready as a Sprint backlog. The team started the Sprint based on committed Sprint backlog items. We have a task board ready for the team to update task status and the Burndown chart to track the team to complete the work in a Sprint.

In this chapter, we will cover the following points:

- How to complete a Sprint
- Working with unfinished Sprint backlog
- Viewing the Sprint report
- Viewing the completed backlog
- Completing an Epic

Completing a Sprint

The team works hard during the course of the Sprint to complete the Sprint backlog items. The Burndown chart shows the regular progress of the team and how the backlog burns over the course of the Sprint. At the end of the Sprint, the team needs to get ready for the Sprint review or demo. And finally, the team completes the Sprint backlog.

While working on the backlog items, the team finishes the technical tasks created during the Sprint. Multiple team members work on different technical tasks for a Story. During the course of the Sprint, we also need to mark the Story as completed or done. While working on the task board in GreenHopper, if you are completing the last technical task for a Story, it allows you to change status for the parent task or Story also.

To change the status of a Story during the course of the Sprint once it is done (when you mark the last technical task as done), you can also mark the Story as done.

As shown in the preceding screenshot, you can choose to mark the parent task as done once you complete the last technical task on the task board. The completion of technical tasks and burn of estimation hours also needs to update the parent issues to be marked as done.

The team has now completed all the Story and issues committed for the Sprint. It is time to complete the Sprint. To end a Sprint in GreenHopper, go to your team's Agile board and click on the **Work** link. Select your active Sprint and click on **Complete Sprint** button.

As shown in the preceding screenshot, the Sprint name and timelines are also displayed when you complete the Sprint.

While completing a Sprint, parent issues are counted in total number of issues, the subtasks, or technical tasks for the Story or issues are automatically included in the Sprint as part of completed backlog. As shown in following screenshot, while completing the Sprint, it displays the total number of issues completed for the Sprint.

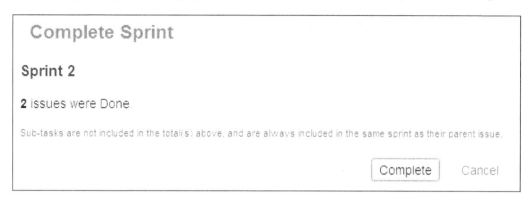

Once you click on the **Complete** button, all the issues from **Work** mode will be moved. Your Sprint will be marked as completed and you will be moved to Sprint report to see the list of issues completed in that Sprint.

Working with unfinished Sprint backlog

There can be scenarios when a team is not able to complete the Sprint backlog. There can be some Stories or issues not completed during the span of the Sprint. When you mark a Sprint as completed, GreenHopper allows you to move back the unfinished Sprint backlog items back to the product backlog.

As shown in the preceding screenshot, while completing a Sprint, it clearly displays the count of unfinished items in the Sprint which will be returned to backlog.

There can be cases when you have completed all the tasks for a Story but the parent issue is not marked as done. You need to also mark the parent Story or issue as done before completing the Sprint, otherwise it will be moved back to the product backlog.

While ending the Sprint, GreenHopper notifies you the list of Story for which the team has completed all the tasks, but it is not yet marked as completed.

Complete Sprint

Sprint 2

2 issues were Done.
1 incomplete issue will be returned to the top of the backlog.

Sub-tasks are not included in the total(s) above, and are always included in the same sprint as their parent issue.

 The following issues, which have all their sub-tasks done, will be returned to the backlog as they are not yet complete:

- APM-24

As shown in the preceding screenshot, while completing the Sprint, it displays the list of the issues which need to be marked as done for which all subtasks are already done.

Mark the Story as completed and proceed to end the Sprint. You can use the Work keyboard shortcut to directly close a Story on the work board.

Viewing the Sprint report

Once you mark the Sprint as completed, it will automatically take you to the Sprint report screen.

The Sprint report shows details for the work done for a particular Sprint. The Sprint report consists of the following two parts:

- The chart displaying the Sprint Burndown information, and how the work was burnt over the span of the Sprint.
- The list of Sprint backlog items completed during the Sprint. You can click on the issue key for the completed backlog items to see the details.

Viewing the completed backlog

Once the Sprint is completed, you cannot reopen it. You can only view the completed Sprint backlog items through the Sprint report. To view the completed Sprint backlog items, go to your team Agile board and click on the **Report** link. Select **Sprint Report** from the drop-down list, as shown in the following screenshot:

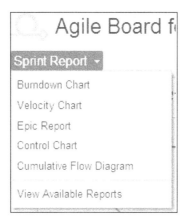

To view the Sprint report for all the completed Sprints, select the relevant Sprint from the Sprint selection dropdown.

As shown in the preceding screenshot, the dropdown will display the list of all the closed and completed Sprints. Once you select the Sprint, the Sprint report will list all the completed Sprint backlog items during that Sprint.

As shown in the preceding screenshot, the details of the Sprint backlog items are displayed on the screen. To see the issue details, click on the issue key link and the issue details will be displayed in the Jira view.

Each completed issue in a Sprint in the Jira view will also display your board details related to the issue. As shown in the following screenshot, the Agile panel displays corresponding Epic and Sprint details for an issue.

From Jira view, you can see the details for the completed backlog, as to which Sprint the issue was completed and which Epic the Story belongs to.

Completing an Epic

An Epic is a big functionality of a product which is further broken down into stories. Stories are completed during a Sprint. Usually an Epic spans over multiple Sprints to get completed.

To see the details of an Epic, go to your team's Agile board. On the **Plan** mode, you will see the **Epics** panel. Click on the Epic under the **Epics** panel for which you want to see the current status.

The **Epics** panel displays your Epic's current status. As shown in the preceding screenshot, it is clear that all the issues assigned to the Epic are now complete and you can also mark the Epic as completed.

To mark the Epic as completed, click on **Mark as Done** in the drop-down selection option, as shown in the following screenshot:

Once you mark an Epic as done, it will no longer be available in the Epics panel. You will only be able to see the Epic details in the Epic Report screen.

Summary

In this chapter, we covered how to mark a Sprint as completed. We covered how to handle the unfinished issues in a Sprint. We also learned to mark issues as done for all tasks already completed, and how to move back the unfinished backlog items to backlog.

We learned to generate the Sprint report on completion of a Sprint. The generated Sprint report helped us to understand team's work Burndown chart for the just ended Sprint in comparison to earlier Sprints. We can always have a complete list of items completed in a Sprint from Sprint report.

We also covered how to end an Epic which automatically generates the Epic report for us. The generated Epic report displays how a particular functionality has been completed over a span of possibly multiple Sprints. In the next chapter, we will be covering generating Epic Report in detail.

In the upcoming chapters, we will be covering how to generate Agile project reports such as Velocity report, Control chart, Cumulative flow diagram, and so on.

8
Project Reporting Using Charts

Agile core values and principles are based on, and support, visibility and collaboration. In any traditional project or Agile project the stakeholders, management, and the team deserves and needs visibility on the project status, roadmap, and the added business value over time.

This chapter covers Agile project reporting and different reports and charts which can be generated. The user will be able to calculate team velocity, check cycle time for an issue to remove the bottlenecks in the system, a particular functionality/Epic completion report, and how the whole of the project backlog is progressing over a period of time.

The following topics will be covered:

- Agile project reporting
- Working with velocity charts
- Working with epic reports
- Working with control charts
- Working with a cumulative flow diagrams

By the end of this chapter, the user will be able to understand the different project reports and charts provided by GreenHopper.

Agile Project Reporting

In the traditional project management, organizations spend big amounts on project reporting and have dedicated people to monitor them. The efforts spent in accommodating and maintaining the fine-grained details of tasks to have minimum risk on the success of the project have lead to the rigorous nature of the project reporting.

In Agile, the concept of *just enough* or *barely sufficient* documentation also applies to the project reporting part. Different Agile methodologies may have different standards and artifacts to report the status of an Agile project. In Scrum, commonly we need reporting for following things:

- **Product backlog** describes how the whole product backlog is progressing across Sprints, how much backlog has been completed, and how much backlog is still remaining to be completed. Looking at the remaining and completed backlog items, we know how many feature requirements are still to be completed by the team and the road map to complete the same. To map to the traditional approach of reporting, the product backlog consists of a full list of feature requests which are required to release a product.

- **Sprint backlog** are the committed backlog items to be delivered or already delivered in a Sprint. The Sprint backlog informs what features have been delivered in each Sprint and how many Sprints it took for a functionality/epic to get delivered. Regular prioritization and adoption to team velocity helps in better reporting on the Sprint backlog and also in incremental delivery of the product backlog.

  Based on measurement unit for a team, Sprint backlog is used to know the team velocity. Team velocity is further used for Sprint mapping and release planning. The product road map is designed based on the calculated delivery capacity of the team, which adopts the changes very well.

- **The Burndown chart** is used to report the team trends during iteration to deliver a Sprint backlog. The simple work of a Burndown chart is to represent how a team is doing over the span of a Sprint. It clearly reports the team progress and bottlenecks in the system for continuous improvements.

From the Agile project management point of view, the regular check and follow-up on the team Burndown chart is very important. Team, Product Owner, Scrum Master, and stakeholders all can have a quick look at the Burndown chart to get indication of the Sprint.

- **Increment and changes**: It is sometimes useful to report what backlog has already been completed and what changes have been done during the span of Sprint. The completed backlog items help to report on how a particular functionality has been delivered over the span of different sprints. The changes report, depending on the requirements, can help to understand if changes' too much of the Sprint backlog affects team focus.

Reporting in GreenHopper

To access the reporting information and different available charts in GreenHopper, go to your team Agile board and click on the **Report** link.

GreenHopper supports the following charts to report the status for your board:

- **Burndown chart**: This shows the Sprint backlog status and the work left over the span of the Sprint. The measurement units are as configured in the estimation statistics.

- **Sprint report**: This shows Sprint backlog items information for a completed Sprint. The detailed view of burndown chart and the sprint backlog items are also displayed.

- **Epic report**: This shows progress of an epic over the span of different sprints, the status of completion, and incomplete issues in an epic.

- **Velocity chart**: This shows the team velocity for completed sprints, the number of estimated points covered or completed in each Sprint.

- **Control chart**: This shows the cycle time for each issue and how long each status in the workflow state took to change to the next state.

- **Cumulative flow diagram**: This shows the backlog flow of completed and remaining backlog items during the product timelines.

We have already covered working with the Burndown chart, Sprint reports, and Epic reports in the earlier chapters. We will be covering here in detail the remaining available reporting options.

Working with velocity chart

Velocity represents the amount of work done in a particular sprint. The amount of work is represented by the estimation measurement unit for the team. The measurement unit for velocity is same as the estimation statistics selected for your estimation process.

To view your current configuration for **Estimation Statistics**, go to your team board. Under the **Tools** action, click on **Configure** and select the **Estimation** tab.

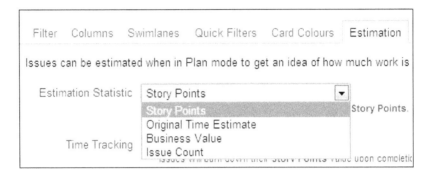

As shown in the preceding screenshot, the following options are available for the estimation based on which the team velocity will be derived:

- **Story Points**: If the estimation measurement unit is Story points, the velocity chart will represent the number of Story points completed in a particular Sprint

- **Original Time Estimate**: If the measurement unit is hours, the velocity chart will represent the number of hours of estimated work completed in a Sprint

- **Business Value**: If measurement unit is business value, the velocity chart will represent the number of business values delivered in a particular Sprint

- **Issue Count**: If issue count is the estimation measurement unit, the velocity is represented as the number of stories or issues completed in a Sprint

Based on your selected estimation measurement unit, the velocity chart is automatically generated for your board.

To view the velocity chart, go to your team board, click on the **Report** link, and select the **Velocity Chart** to view it as shown in the following screenshot:

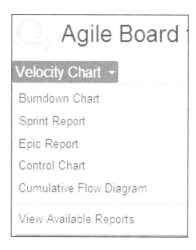

As shown in the preceding screenshot, it shows you the team velocity over different sprints. Teams will use the same number to commit for the work in the next Sprint.

As each Agile team is different from each other, each team has its own strength and way of working. The productivity and way of working for each team differs from each other. The biggest challenge for any team working in an Agile way is to find the correct velocity. It does take some course of initial sprints to finally find the correct team velocity. The velocity figure gets corrected as the team finishes more Sprints. Velocity is calculated as an average of the number of sprints finished.

The team and product owner work together to analyze the team velocity and take the data from velocity chart during the planning phase to plan the Sprint backlog better. Over a period of time, looking at data for multiple Sprints, you need to watch closely how the team is performing on the committed Sprint backlog items and the actual number of completed items. The numbers will give you a fair idea about whether the team is over-committing or under-committing, or how correct the estimations are. The data is just an indication of something that needs to be looked at and the actual nature of the problem will vary from team to team. The following screenshot shows a velocity chart:

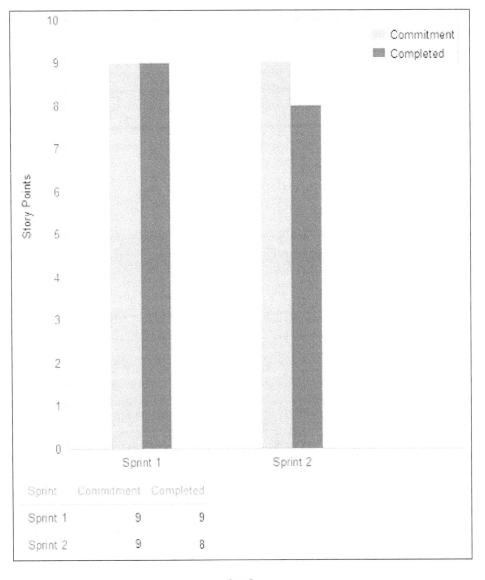

Sprint	Commitment	Completed
Sprint 1	9	9
Sprint 2	9	8

Another aspect of having a regular watch on the team velocity data is to analyze it regularly and work in a way which ensures continuous improvement. Each team needs to see how they can improve the team velocity. Team, Scrum master, and product owner all work together to minimize waste in the process and enable the team to increase on the team velocity working at a sustainable pace.

Working with epic report

Epic is a feature or functionality usually completed over a span of multiple sprints. From a reporting perspective, we need to know how a particular feature was completed over the sprints, how much effort was required for the feature to be completed, and what all issues were a part of the Epic.

To access the epic report, go to your team board, click on the **Report** link and select **Epic Report** from the dropdown. From the list of currently active or open Epics, select the relevant Epic on which you want to generate the report.

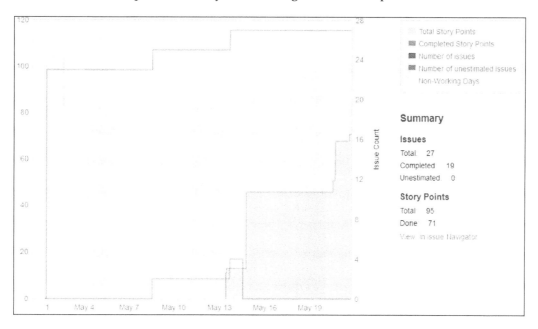

As shown in the preceding screenshot, for a particular Epic, the Epic report shows you the details of the total Story points, the total Story points completed in each sprint, and remaining unfinished issues.

The status report also shows you the list of completed issues for the selected Epic.

Working with control chart

The control chart is a measurement criterion to determine if the process/data under analysis will produce the desired result in future. By examining the data over a period of time, we can analyze if it is running at a sustainable pace or not. By looking at huge variations in the data, we will be able to decide if we need to introspect the process or flow, or not.

To access the control chart, go to your team board, click on the **Report** link and select **Control Chart**.

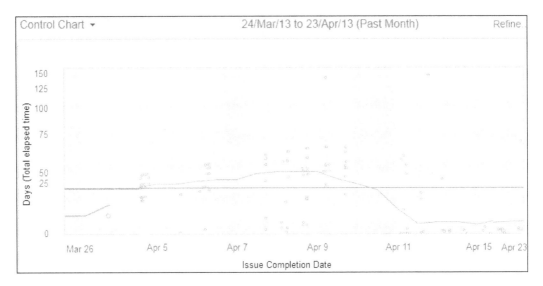

The preceding screenshot shows a sample control chart for an Agile team. The x axis represents the time (number of days) for an issue to be in single workflow state, and the y axis represents the time frame.

The statistical analysis helps us to introspect the process from a planning perspective. The aggregate mean and standard deviation of the time helps us to focus on bottlenecks and see if any action is required or not.

The cycle time for an issue represents how much time it spends in a particular state. The cycle time in each flow state can help us to examine the bottleneck in each state of the flow. If one of the states is taking too much time for an issue to move to the next, the focus can be to improve cycle time in a particular workflow state.

If any of the issue state variation is too much, as shown in the preceding screenshot, we may have to analyze special cases, why it happened and how it can be avoided in future. Hover over any node in the control chart to see a pop up of the issue key, time in progress, and cycle time. Analyzing the control chart can help us to improve the cycle time and also in continuous improvement of the process to achieve maximum productivity.

You can control the **Report Timeframe** for the chart, by selecting the relevant timelines, as shown in the following screenshot:

You can control the date range for the generated data to analyze how the backlog items behave over a period of time. The generated data can help you to analyze how much time each issue was taking during the start of the process and how long it took to come to a sustainable pace or the desired level.

If you want to focus on a selected portion of the backlog to analyze how the filtered backlog items perform over the span of time, you can use the refine functionality to filter the data better. As shown in the following screenshot, click on the **Refine...** link.

You can filter the data further based on different available selection criteria. You can select specific **Columns** of your task board representing mapped issue status with the columns. You can also select horizontal grouping values as **Swimlanes** to generate reports. Also, you can select configured **Quick Filters** to filter your chart data further.

Working with a cumulative flow diagram

The cumulative flow diagram is a graphical representation of the issues in different flow states over a period of time. It represents the work accomplished over time. The Burndown chart is drawn for incremental backlog over the span of a Sprint and the cumulative flow diagram is plotted over the span of a release cycle.

To access the cumulative flow diagram, go to your team board, click on the **Report** link and select **Cumulative Flow Diagram**.

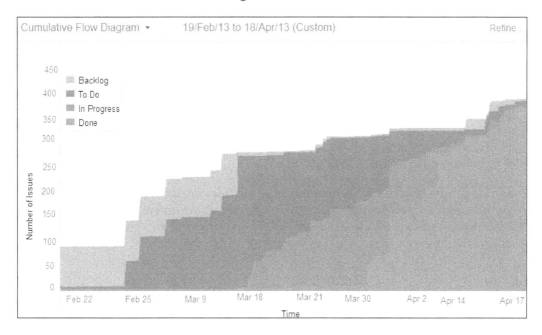

As shown in the preceding screenshot, the cumulative flow diagram is plotted displaying the initial "to do" backlog items and how the work is accomplished over time.

The cumulative flow diagram clearly shows the work which still needs to be done, the work in progress,, and completed work over time.

You can select **Report timeframe** for the diagram by selecting a specific date range as shown in preceding screenshot. You can also use the refine functionality to filter the data further.

Summary

In this chapter, we covered the reporting options for an Agile project, the typical Agile reports and charts required for an Agile project which covered product backlog reports, Sprint backlog reports, cycle time, and cumulative flow diagrams.

We also covered the velocity chart which indicates the team capacity to deliver business value in a sprint. The Epic report shows the functionality details in terms of effort required, total number of issues, and already finished issues for the Epic.

The control chart allowed us to analyze the cycle time for the issues and enabled us to focus on the bottlenecks and improving them. The cumulative flow diagram displayed the flow of work over time.

In the upcoming chapter, we will be covering the Kanban system in detail. We will cover how to use GreenHopper in detail to manage your Kanban team, create a Kanban board, update task board for the Kanban team, and generate reports for the Kanban team.

9
Managing Kanban Team with GreenHopper

Kanban is a well-known **Lean** process commonly used in manufacturing and in software development as well. Kanban is about focusing on visualizing the flow of work and limiting the work in progress for smooth and continuous delivery.

In this chapter, we will cover:

- The Kanban system
- Push model versus Pull model
- Kanban for software delivery and services team
- Creating the Kanban board in GreenHopper
- Configuring columns and limiting work in progress
- Creating Swimlanes for the Kanban team
- Ranking issues on the Kanban board
- Reporting for the Kanban team

Kanban system

Kanban is a signal card used in any pull system. It is about visual flow of value through the system by eliminating waste using a pull system based on limiting work in progress and improving the flow process continuously. It is based on different Lean principles such as delivering customer value, eliminating waste, pull systems, and continuous improvement.

Kanban reveals the bottlenecks in the continuous delivery system. By limiting the work in progress, you will reveal the bottlenecks in the system and will be able to take action to resolve them.

Before using the Kanban boards, we need to understand the basic difference between pull and push models in the delivery system.

Push model versus Pull model

The old methodology usually follows the push model where the work is pushed or assigned to a team member or a team. Usually the team leader or manager assigns tasks to different team members as shown in the following diagram:

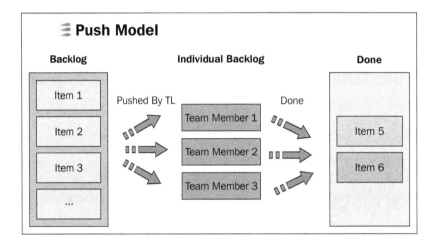

There are multiple issues with the push model, such as a lot of waste in the process, individual backlog burdens, no team collaboration, no clear visibility in bottlenecks in the system, and work may get stuck at different levels in the system.

A typical pull model looks as shown in the following diagram:

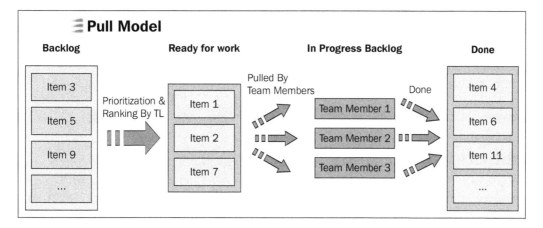

Some of the pull system benefits are:

- It supports the continuous flow of work
- Work is done as a team
- There is a clear indication of state of work
- Work in progress is limited for each status
- There is a lesser burden on individual backlog
- It allows better planning and prioritization of work
- It allows improved continuous delivery

Kanban system implements the pull model for continuous delivery by eliminating the waste and focusing on continuous improvement.

Kanban for software delivery and the services team

Kanban has been adopted as a favored software development process where the teams deliver continuous business value. Mostly Kanban is used for the team where we have continuous flow of work and some clear examples of such teams are as follows:

Maintenance team

The maintenance team works on maintaining a project, where bug fixes and improvements for the system need to be done regularly and based on prioritization, the fixes are delivered.

Operations team

The operations team maintains a system from an operations perspective, where system maintenance activities and system improvements are always in pipeline. One classic example is the site operations team which maintains the healthy state of a site along with regular improvement projects.

Infrastructure/Network team

The infrastructure/Network team regularly supports IT related user queries or ticket requests and also works on infrastructure improvement projects.

Services/Support team

The s Services/Support team handles end user customer support tickets.

A typical board for the continuous flow would look as shown in the following diagram. You have a list of **Goals** where the entire product backlog will reside. The categorization of the backlog, as to whether it is an incident ticket/production issue or regular support ticket is up to you. The next state is the prioritization of goals into **Queue** for team members to pick the tasks.

Each team member picks up items from a queue based on priority and starts working on that. The issues in the incident list and so on are always on the top of list. The team will pick those as soon as any issue pops up. The following diagram shows a Kanban board:

Once the issues in progress are finished, they are marked as done. Each column has a limit for how many issues you can pick in one state.

Creating a Kanban board in GreenHopper

We have a fair idea by now how a Kanban system works. We will be covering further how to use GreenHopper to manage such Kanban teams. GreenHopper has inbuilt support for Kanban system to create a board, limit work in progress, and track and report Kanban teams.

To create a Kanban board in GreenHopper, navigate to **Agile** tab and click on **Getting Started**. Select the option of **Kanban Managed Flow**. Click on the link **Create a new Kanban board** in the next step.

As shown in the preceding screenshot, enter the board name and select relevant projects for which you want to create the Kanban board.

If you don't have a project in place yet, you can click on the **create a project and board** link to create both project and board. Once you are ready with your board, you will be directed to the work mode of your Kanban board.

Configuring columns and limiting work in progress

To view the currently configured columns for your Kanban board, go to the **Tools** action, click on **Configure** and select the **Columns** tab. The screen will show you existing statuses and column mappings for your work board.

Check the **Simplified Workflow** status on your screen. If you had created a project and Kanban board from the **Getting Started** page, the **GreenHopper Simplified Workflow** will be automatically available to you as shown in the following screenshot.

We will be adding a new status and column to our work flow here. A new column **Queue** will be added to store the prioritized list of backlog items.

To add a new status, click on the **Add Status** button and enter status name as Queue. To add a new column, click on the **Add Column** button and enter column name as Queue.

As shown in the preceding screenshot, the following columns have been configured for the Kanban board:

- **Goals**: This lists the items which, on creation in the backlog, will automatically be listed here. This will act as the complete list of backlog items.
- **Queue**: This includes the prioritized list of items which is ready for teams to pull from.
- **In Progress**: This includes list of issues which are currently in progress state.
- **Done**: This includes the issues which have been marked as done.

Limiting the work in progress is another functionality you can configure for each column. You can add constraints on the column values.

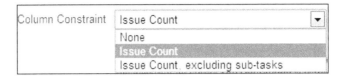

The configuration as shown in the preceding screenshot will allow you to add constraints on a column based on the number of issues that can be in a particular column.

To apply constraints on the column, edit the minimum and maximum value using inline editing functionality in the column as shown in the following screenshot:

For example, there should always be items in queue for the teams to work upon. The maximum number of issues that can be in progress at a particular moment can be as per the configured value.

As soon as the constraints are violated, the column colors will automatically change to notify you that something needs to be done. If the minimum value for the constraint is violated, the box will turn yellow, if the maximum value is violated the box will turn red.

The constraint values are clearly visible on your work board as shown in the following screenshot:

To remove bottlenecks in the continuous delivery system, always keep an eye on the constraint value for your Kanban board.

Creating Swimlane for Kanban team

A Swimlane is a means of grouping and categorizing the issues together on work board. For a Kanban team, prioritization and grouping of backlog issues is very important. The team needs to know which issues are of higher priority, the clear distinction between regular support tickets and improvements, and so on, to ensure that work on the backlog item is much more streamlined and smooth.

To access existing Swimlanes for your board, go to the **Tools** action, click on **Configure** and select the **Swimlanes** tab.

Check your current Swimlanes settings, select **Queries** to take advantage of advanced **Jira Query Language (JQL)** to create Swimlanes, as shown in the preceding screenshot.

Some examples of typical Swimlanes for Kanban team based on current project settings and JQL are as displayed in following screenshot:

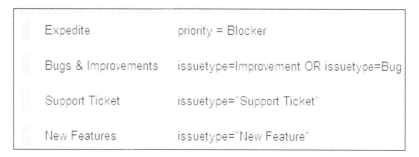

For example, suppose you want to **Expedite** all blocker issues, but you also want to separate out the new feature requirements from regular bugs and improvements.

The grouping of these issues based on Swimlanes will be clearly reflected on your work board. Swimlanes will provide you with horizontal categorization of your issues on your work board as shown in following screenshot:

Teams can now control the flow of prioritized and high value backlog items in a much better way.

Ranking issues on the Kanban work board

To rank issues on the Kanban work board, use the drag-and-drop functionality. You should be able to move items on a column in vertical direction to rank them, as shown in the following screenshot.

The first prioritization is based on the grouping and categorization of issues. Combining issues which need to be expedited are of higher priority in queue than the regular bugs and tickets. For each Swimlane, you should be able to move items in the same column to rank them.

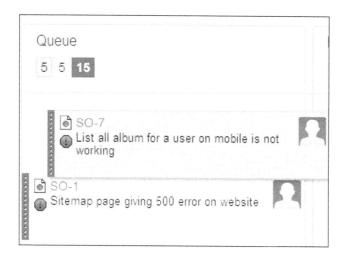

Reporting for the Kanban team

GreenHopper provides the following reporting tools and charts available for Kanban teams which can help them in monitoring and continuous improvement:

Cumulative Flow Diagram

To view the cumulative flow diagram, select **Report** mode and click on **Cumulative Flow Diagram**.

The cumulative flow diagram will display the incoming work which still needs to be done, work still in progress, and work that is already finished. Balancing the work that still needs to be done and controlling the work in progress can clearly show if a team is capable of handling all the incoming work or when the team will be able to finish the piled-up work.

The detailed cumulative flow diagram has already been covered in previous chapters.

Control chart

To view the cumulative flow diagram, select the **Report** mode and click on **Control Chart**.

For Kanban teams, the cycle time is very important. Analyzing the cycle time helps the team to focus on the bottleneck in the whole process flow. Reducing the cycle time is one of the challenges for the Kanban teams and it becomes part of continuously improving it.

The detailed control chart has already been covered in previous chapters.

Summary

We discussed the basic concepts of Kanban process. We covered the differences between the push and pull model to deliver the business value.

We created Kanban board in GreenHopper to get started with the Kanban board. We added separate statuses and columns on the Kanban board to map to the Kanban team requirements which allows prioritizing the items to put in queue.

We covered each column constraint to control the flow of work in each state and to visualize the same if column limits for work exceeds.

We also covered the prioritization of items on the Kanban board and to generate different reporting for your Kanban team.

A
Continuous Improvement

The traditional approach of capturing the improvements for the project execution used to be at the end of the project in order to improve the future projects. One of the core aspects of Agile is the idea of continuous improvement while you are currently working on the project.

The Agile way of improvements for lessons learned is a deliberate and frequent approach. It ensures that the team regularly considers adaptation and improvement which makes it part of their normal way of working. Some of the common forms of improvements are as follows:

- Retrospective
- Knowledge sharing
- Process improvements
- Wiki integration
- Testing collaboration
- Team communication
- Continuous integration
- Technical debt
- Code reviews
- Reporting and Dashboard
- Notifications (Email/SMS)
- IDE integration
- Plugins

Retrospective

The Sprint retrospective is a process that examines what went well, what needs improvements, and continuous improvement commitments for the next Sprint. The use of a tracking tool such as **Jira/GreenHopper** provides the historic data to look back and assess each Sprint.

Knowledge sharing

Agile urges the team to be a self-organized team rather than a managed team. The mutual code ownership and team collaboration demands a lot of knowledge sharing within the team. Either it is domain knowledge or technical knowledge, each team uses different ways to achieve results. Documentation of critical functionality, separate knowledge sharing sessions, and pair programming helps to achieve these results. The flexible and customizable nature of Jira/GreenHopper allows you to plan and track these activities.

Process improvements

Each team uses the set of Agile practices which fits the team best. The hybrid nature of the Agile way allows delivery of best business value within team and business boundaries. GreenHopper is configurable to best fit your Agile team needs. Based on your team requirements and feedback points during retrospective analysis after each Sprint, you can configure GreenHopper to adapt to the process improvements.

Wiki integration

Agile suggests *just enough* or *barely sufficient* documentation. The documentation may vary from end user documentation, API documentation, technical design, or third party integration. Atlassian wiki solution **Confluence** (`http://www.atlassian.com/software/confluence/overview/team-collaboration-software`) provides a rich document management system that integrates deeply with Jira/GreenHopper. Teams can choose to store additional documentation information on the wiki keeping backlog with concise information only.

Testing collaboration

All members of the Scrum team are responsible for quality, testers, developers, and product owners. Usually each Agile team has an Agile tester responsible for verification and validation of the functional part of the application. We also have a product owner and a stakeholder to perform regression tests and give feedback on meeting acceptance criteria. Jira brings the plugin named **Bonfire** (`http://www.atlassian.com/software/bonfire/overview`) to help the team to coordinate and integrate testing into Jira/GreenHopper. Using the Bonfire plugin, you can coordinate the testing, fixing, and backlog management in a much better way.

Team communication

Communication is the backbone of any of the Agile methodologies, where we say each team member as well as the product owners should be easily accessible for clarification. For distributed teams this also becomes kind of a bottleneck sometimes. The Atlassian group chat tool named **HipChat** (`http://www.atlassian.com/software/hipchat/overview`) helps your team to stay connected. HipChat integrates well with Jira/GreenHopper and other tools by writing issue transitions and tool activities into a HipChat room.

Continuous integration

One of the best practices of continuously integrating the checked in code allows teams to focus on quality of the product and making sure the team works towards potential shippable solution. Atlassian continuous integration solution named **Bamboo** (`http://www.atlassian.com/software/bamboo/overview`) provides a complete release workflow. You can integrate it with Jira/GreenHopper allowing teams to create issues in analyzing any build failure or dependency issues. The nice dashboard and reporting tools gives the additional benefit of analyzing it over period of time.

Technical debt

The nonfunctional requirements for any project are quite practical. The technical debt represents the things which teams would like to improve upon within the code. Each team monitors the list in different ways. You can document the list in wiki and link with Jira to access it quickly. You can also create separate issue types or components to represent the backlog for technical debt.

Code review

To ensure the quality of delivered products, each team follows a code review process differently. Some teams prefer to pair program, some create separate tasks to track formal code reviews, while some use tooling systems to achieve this result. Atlassian solution named **Crucible** (`http://www.atlassian.com/software/crucible/overview`) allows you to conduct peer code reviews much effectively. Jira/GreenHopper allows you to track and manage the process in a much easier way and integrates smoothly with your code repository.

Reporting and dashboard

Easy and flexible reporting and visual display of information, and focusing on only relevant information is the Agile way of doing it. Sufficient reporting capabilities of Jira/GreenHopper, easy integration with other Atlassian suites, and additional features of gadgets allow you to achieve the desired results quickly.

Notifications

The notification capabilities of e-mail or SMS allow your teams to stay notified all the time. Subscriptions to saved filters provide routine notification of JQL queries and watching individual issues provide opt-in notifications upon changes. Additional hooks and plugins for notifications make it easy for both development and operations teams to be notified and relevant actions can be planned accordingly.

IDE integration

The easy integration of tooling systems such as Jira, Bamboo, and Crucible within the IDE can be achieved using **IDE Connector** (`http://www.atlassian.com/software/ide-connectors/overview`). It allows teams to focus on work and less on tooling. Teams can easily integrate these tools with the development environment and each team member stays connected and updated to the changes. This leads to an increase in productivity while minimizing the time spent on waiting significantly.

Plugins

The vast list of additional available plugins for the tooling system allows you to choose and work with the ones suiting best to your team. To name a few, the plugins such as Tempo for timesheet, Issue hierarchy plugin and Charting plugins for reporting, and so on extend Jira/GreenHopper to provide needed features through a vast market place of third party providers.

Index

Kanban team
  reporting 115
  Swimlane, creating 113, 114
keyboard shortcuts, Scrum task board 60
knowledge sharing 118

L

Lean process 105

M

measurement units, Burndown chart 78

O

onDemand 12
organization teams, GreenHopper examples
  IT infrastructure team 15

P

plain mode, Scrum board 29
planning 42
process improvements 118
product backlog 17
product backlog, Scrum artifacts 10
product owner, Scrum team 9
project backlog 25
pull model
  about 107
  benefits 107
push model 106

Q

quick filtering, GreenHopper interface
  features 20
Quick Filters
  about 17, 65
  accessing 66
  adding 66
  creating 66
  displaying 66
  working with 65, 67

R

reporting, for Kanban team
  about 115
  Control chart 116
  Cumulative flow diagram 115
reporting, in GreenHopper
  about 95
  charts 95
report mode, Scrum board 29
reports, Agile project reporting
  Epic report 95
  Sprint report 95
responsiveness, GreenHopper interface
  features 20

S

scope management, for Sprint 80-82
Scrum 8, 16
Scrum artifacts
  about 10
  increment 10
Scrum board
  configuration mode, cancelling 31
  creating 28, 29
  Jira filter configurations 30
  managing 30
  plain mode 29
  report mode 29-31
  switching, between modes 29, 30
  work mode 29
Scrum events
  about 9
  Daily Scrum 9
  Sprint 9
  Sprint planning meeting 9
  Sprint review 9
Scrum master 9
Scrum task board
  about 54
  accessing 55
  column, adding 57
  done status 54

V

velocity 17
Velocity chart
  about 95
  working with 96-99

W

Wiki integration 118
working and non-working days
        configuration
  about 79

non-working days 80
standard working days 79
time zone 79
work mode, Scrum board 29

X

XP (Extreme Programming) 8

Thank you for buying
Agile Project Management with GreenHopper 6 Blueprints

About Packt Publishing

Packt, pronounced 'packed', published its first book *"Mastering phpMyAdmin for Effective MySQL Management"* in April 2004 and subsequently continued to specialize in publishing highly focused books on specific technologies and solutions.

Our books and publications share the experiences of your fellow IT professionals in adapting and customizing today's systems, applications, and frameworks. Our solution based books give you the knowledge and power to customize the software and technologies you're using to get the job done. Packt books are more specific and less general than the IT books you have seen in the past. Our unique business model allows us to bring you more focused information, giving you more of what you need to know, and less of what you don't.

Packt is a modern, yet unique publishing company, which focuses on producing quality, cutting-edge books for communities of developers, administrators, and newbies alike. For more information, please visit our website: www.packtpub.com.

Writing for Packt

We welcome all inquiries from people who are interested in authoring. Book proposals should be sent to author@packtpub.com. If your book idea is still at an early stage and you would like to discuss it first before writing a formal book proposal, contact us; one of our commissioning editors will get in touch with you.

We're not just looking for published authors; if you have strong technical skills but no writing experience, our experienced editors can help you develop a writing career, or simply get some additional reward for your expertise.

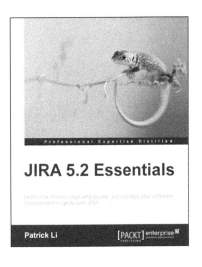

JIRA 5.2 Essentials

ISBN: 978-1-78217-999-3 Paperback: 396 pages

Learn how to track bugs and issues, and manage your software development projects with JIRA

1. Learn how to set up JIRA for software development

2. Effectively manage and handle software bugs and issues

3. Includes updated JIRA content as well as coverage of the popular GreenHopper plugin

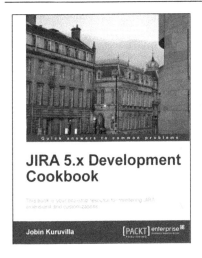

JIRA 5.x Development Cookbook

ISBN: 978-1-78216-908-6 Paperback: 512 pages

This book is your one-stop resource for mastering JIRA extensions and customizations

1. Extend and customize JIRA; work with custom fields, workflows, reports, gadgets, JQL functions, plugins, and more

2. Customize the look and feel of your JIRA user interface by adding new tabs, web items and sections, drop down menus, and more

3. Master JQL (JIRA Query Language) that enables advanced searching capabilities through which users can search for issues in their JIRA instance and then exploit all the capabilities of the issue navigator

Please check **www.PacktPub.com** for information on our titles

Atlassian Confluence 5 Essentials

ISBN: 978-1-84968-952-6   Paperback: 334 pages

Learn how to install, configure, and manage Atlassian Confluence 5 to build an enterprise-grade collaboration platform

1. Create and manage project documentation with Confluence

2. Share and collaborate on documentation between departments and teams

3. Install, configure, manage, and extend Confluence

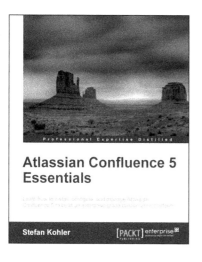

The Professional ScrumMaster's Handbook

ISBN: 978-1-84968-802-4   Paperback: 336 pages

A collection of tips, tricks, and war stories to help the professional ScrumMaster break the chains of traditional organization and management

1. Checklists, questions, and exercises to get you thinking (and acting) like a professional ScrumMaster

2. Presented in a relaxed, jargon-free, personable style

3. Full of ideas, tips, and anecdotes based on real-world experiences

Please check **www.PacktPub.com** for information on our titles

www.ingramcontent.com/pod-product-compliance
Lightning Source LLC
LaVergne TN
LVHW080059070326
832902LV00014B/2316